Young Writers
2004 POETRY CO[...]

ONCE UPON A RHYME

IMAGINATION FOR
A NEW GENERATION

**Poems From
North West England**
Edited by Kelly Oliver

Young Writers

First published in Great Britain in 2005 by:
Young Writers
Remus House
Coltsfoot Drive
Peterborough
PE2 9JX
Telephone: 01733 890066
Website: www.youngwriters.co.uk

All Rights Reserved

© Copyright Contributors 2004

SB ISBN 1 84460 681 3

Foreword

Young Writers was established in 1991 and has been passionately devoted to the promotion of reading and writing in children and young adults ever since. The quest continues today. Young Writers remains as committed to engendering the fostering of burgeoning poetic and literary talent as ever.

This year's Young Writers competition has proven as vibrant and dynamic as ever and we are delighted to present a showcase of the best poetry from across the UK. Each poem has been carefully selected from a wealth of *Once Upon A Rhyme* entries before ultimately being published in this, our twelfth primary school poetry series.

Once again, we have been supremely impressed by the overall high quality of the entries we have received. The imagination, energy and creativity which has gone into each young writer's entry made choosing the best poems a challenging and often difficult but ultimately hugely rewarding task - the general high standard of the work submitted amply vindicating this opportunity to bring their poetry to a larger appreciative audience.

We sincerely hope you are pleased with our final selection and that you will enjoy *Once Upon A Rhyme Poems From North West England* for many years to come.

Contents

Arnot Community School, Liverpool
Anya Gillin (10)	1
Megan Cavanagh (10)	1
Kayla Thompson (9)	2
Ryan Landry (10)	2
Nikita Aspinwall (10)	3
Rebecca Sealeaf (9)	3
Daniel Melia (10)	3
Mark James (9)	4
Billiejo Fairclough (10)	4
Debra Bell (9)	5
Ashleigh Buckley (9)	5
Katie Lau (10)	6
Abbie Davies (9)	6

Blacklow Brow Primary School, Huyton
Jenna Potter (8)	6
Sean Givnan (10)	7
Kyle Limbert (11)	7
Luke Birchall (8)	7
Stephanie Weston (10)	8
Liam Lannigan (11)	8
Jazmine Moody (10)	9
Louis Weston (10)	9
Laura Gilmore (10)	10
Stephanie McVey (10)	10
Sophie Gaffney (10)	11
Jonathan Daly (10)	11
Emma Clarke (8)	11
Megan Roper (9)	12
Millie Weston (8)	12
Ellie Wallace (9)	12
James Shone (8)	13
Hope Whewell (8)	13
Brittany Heyes (8)	13
Simon Ridgway (9)	14
Abbie Wood (8)	14
Ruth Peach (8)	14
Abbie McCormack (9)	15

Naomi Birbeck (8)	15
Russell Taylor (8)	15
Jessica Harvey (9)	16
Heidi Ridgway (7)	16
Charlie Vidamour (7)	16
Daniel Turnley (9)	17
Lewis Cox (7)	17
Patrik Taylor (7)	17
Stephanie Wood (7)	18
Jamie White (7)	18
Matthew Morris (7)	18
Catherine Arnold (7)	19
Callum Reardon (7)	19
David Murphy (7)	19
Haaris Moynihan (8)	20
Matthew Thomalla (7)	20
Mollie Christopher (7)	20
Olivia Rose Hood (7)	21
Rachel Benbow (8)	21
Chloe Webster (7)	21
Maria Blanchflower (9)	22
Alexandra Weston (8)	22
Matthew Donnelly (9)	23
Ross Swift (9)	23
Philippa Gee (9)	24
Emma Gibson (9)	24
Daniel Daly (9)	24
Alex Gynane (9)	25
Daniel Dacey (9)	25
Katie Mahoney (9)	25

Carr Mill Primary School, St Helens

Cerys Edden (9)	26
Kirsty Clayton (9)	26
Robert Smith Latham (9)	26
Linda Lee (9)	27
Jessica Masters (9)	27
Darren Thelwell (9)	27
Samantha Pye (9)	28
Jordan Hale (9)	28
Robert Lever (9)	28

Marissa Donnellan (9) — 29
Katrina Hilton (9) — 29
Kieron Dixon (9) — 29
Callum Gray (9) — 30

Clifford Holroyde Centre of Expertise, Liverpool
Kieran Cunningham (10) — 30

Higher Bebington Junior School, Wirral
Katrina Burns (9) — 30
Abbi Penketh (9) — 31
Jamie-Lee Sadler (10) — 31
Emma Sadler (7) — 31
Matthew Herbison (7) — 32
Calista Dufton-Kelly (10) — 32
George Anderson (8) — 33
Niamh Meehan (7) — 33
Jenny Cook (10) — 34
Eleanor Meehan (10) — 35
Rachel Williams (11) — 35
Ben Savage (8) — 36
Sarah Taylor (10) — 36
Sean Cavanagh (10) — 37
Haidee Booth (9) & Dayna Booth (7) — 37
Jessica Crane (11) — 38
Alex Butler (9) — 38
Jessica Morris (7) — 39
Charlotte Moore (9) — 39
Natalie Taylor (8) — 39
Paul Cavanagh (7) — 40
Katrina Ryan (8) — 40
Daniel Siddorn (9) — 40

Holy Trinity CE Primary School, Wirral
Jessie Evans (11) — 41
Jack Howse (7) — 41
Emily McIlroy (8) — 42
Hannah Colley (9) — 42
Ellie Davies (8) — 43
Bradley Done (11) — 44

Anna Turner (7)	44
Joe Smith (10)	45
Hannah Waddington (7)	45
Oscar Reddrop (10)	46
Jenna Lavelle (7)	46
Megan Edge (8)	47
Simon Dore (7)	47
Emma Fairbanks (10)	48
Maria Manley (10)	49
Chelsea Morris (8)	50
Philip McIlroy (10)	50
Daisy Manning (8)	51
Kelly Sinnett (9)	51
Lorin Thompson (10)	52
Olivia Burnie (9)	52
Laura Burton (8)	53
Rosie Evans (9)	53
Ben Fitzpatrick (9)	54
Erica Daley (9)	54
Oliver Jones (9)	55
Chloe Trollone (9)	55
Isobel Thierry-Simpson (9)	56
Alexandra Campbell (8)	56
Joel Thompson (8)	57
Niamh Roberts (8)	57
Nicola Alty (8)	57
Kelly Manley (8)	58

Longton Lane Community Primary School, Rainhill

Jordan Gore (8)	58
Caitlin Hodgkinson (8)	58
Fiona Pye (8)	59
Alex Storey (8)	59
Owen Briers (8)	59
Hannah Morton (8)	60
Rhian Keating (8)	60
Erin Gray (8)	61
Adam Prescott (8)	61
Daniel Vickers (8)	62

Newton-le-Willows Primary School, Newton-le-Willows

Adam Whitfield	62
Aarron Rae (10)	62
Sasha Sandford	63
Lauren Bate	63
Sophie Gregory (10)	63
Jasmine Squires	64
Laura Poultney	64
Perry Brockley	64
Lauren Walsh	65
Alison Wood	65
Alex Findley (10)	65
Thomas Hallett (10)	66
Sam Tedjini (10)	66
Liam Haselden (10)	66
Natasha Livsey	67
Samuel Rahaman (10)	67
Keanu Court	67
Ashley Murphy	68
Michael Higgins (9)	68
Jack Skelton	68
Leah Astbury (9)	69
Aleesha Meadows (9)	69
Rebecca Chesworth (10)	69
Estee Voong	70
Daye Hardman	70
Rachel Winstanley (9)	70
Megan Kavanagh (7)	71
Joseph Forshaw (9)	71
Aiyshia Seebue (7)	71
Bradley Swift (9)	72
Joseph Botsford (9)	72
Samuel Munro Lyon (8)	72
Helen Robinson (9)	73
Lucy Woods (9)	73
Rowan Lawrence	73
Hannah Riding	73
Jamie Boyle (9)	74
Nicola Unsworth (8)	74
Abigail Byrne (8)	74
Adam Hazeldine	74

Adam Mellor (9)	75
Louise Culling (7)	75
Siobhan Carney	75
Rebecca Griffiths	75
Jessica Judge (9)	76
Adam Bond	76
Christopher Cunliffe (9)	76
Georgia Ivanovic (9)	77
Logan Newsome (9)	77
James Parkinson	77
Scott Clare	78
Cory Plant (9)	78
Nicole Vero	78
Bethany Furbey (9)	79
Jamie Seddon (9)	79
Asher Barry (9)	79
Nathan Anderson (9)	80
Hayley Grierson	80
Jade Waring (10)	80
Adam Philip (7)	81
Laura Roberts (9)	81
Malcolm Austin	81
Nathon Hollis (7)	82
Paige Melia (11)	82
Nathan Smith (10)	82
Nancy Bennett	83
Lucy Platt (10)	83
Kealan R-Smith (10)	83
Scott Reilly (10)	84
Adam Roberts (10)	84
Lauren Kilshaw (11)	84
Katie Hovvels (11)	85
Charlotte Stein (11)	85
Lucy Crean (10)	85
Chelsey Oakes	86
Bethany Vizard	86
Kayleigh Aspinwall (11)	86
Danielle Williams	87
Tiffany Eccles	87
Sarah Gordon-Simpson	87
Louise Clare (10)	88

St Columba's Catholic Primary School, Huyton
Megan Canning (9) — 88
Lea Courtney, Liam Metcalfe (8) Michael Scales (10) — 88
Rebecca Darracott (10) — 89
Nicola Sullivan & Lauren Sothern (10) — 89
Kimberley Dooley, Natalie Dooley & Lauren Cassells (10) — 90
Nicola Jones & Jessica Gardner (10) — 90
Laura Fitzsimmons (9) — 91
Joe Bennett & Kyle Hughes (10) — 91
Amanda Coughlan (10) — 92

Sunnymede School, Southport
Charlotte Atherton (10) — 92
Faye Liley (9) — 93
George Alexander (9) — 93
Alasdair Mitchell (9) — 94
Grace Robertson (9) — 94
Ellie Mawdsley (9) — 95
Giles Mawdsley (10) — 95
Bethany Ferns (10) — 96
Michael Speed (10) — 96
Lewis Houlgrave (10) — 97
Aidan Harrison (9) — 97
Thomas Griffin-Lea (10) — 98
Jack Morris-Holland (10) — 98
Adam Galley (10) — 98
Joe Mansour (10) — 99
Adam Finnigan (10) — 99
Edward Rigby (10) — 99
Jack Cope (9) — 100
Georgina Williams (10) — 100
Cassie Kelly-Donoghue (9) — 101

Waterloo Primary School, Liverpool
Jonathan Wild (7) — 101
Megan Ward (8) — 102
Holly McGhee (8) — 102
Georgia Smith (9) — 102
Aimee Hughes (8) — 103
Ben Cook (8) — 103

Rebecca Swinnerton (8)	103
Melissa Clarke (8)	104
Valerie Anirah (8)	104
Katy Maybury (11)	104
Alex Kershaw (10)	105
Sam Cook (10)	105
Kelsey Cunnah (8)	105
Molly O'Callaghan (10)	106
Karim Benallal (10)	106
Natalie Brazendale (10)	106
Rachel Bellamy (10)	107
Joanne Tasker (10)	107
Luke Macaulay (10)	107
Hannah Stevens (8)	108
Andy Gilbert (11)	108
Emma Brie (10)	108
Ryan Maybury (7)	109
Leah Bryant (7)	109
Ellen Ashcroft (7)	109
Lee Clarke (7)	110
Katie McCollah (7)	110
Stephanie Joy (7)	111
Rosie Biggar (7)	111
Lauren Burdell (7)	112
Daniel Ritson (7)	112
Kieran Jones (8)	113
Bronwyn Richardson (7)	113
Alexandra Holmes (7)	114
Robbie Gourlay (8)	114
Olivia Morris (7)	115
Josh Martin (7)	115
Michael Wainwright (9)	116
Andrew Jones (10)	116
Matthew Liggett (7)	116
Abbie Weedall (9)	117
Luke Williams (8)	117
Mark Lythgoe (9)	117
Scott Pursall (7)	118
Abbie Larkin (8)	118
Jack McCourt (8)	118
Emma Foy (8)	119
Toni Dolan (8)	119

Jake Strickland (9) 119
Shannon Traynier 120
Jenny Glen (8) 120
Jamie Woodward (9) 120
Rachel Buckley (8) 121
Rachel Gilbert 121
Abby Scott (8) 121
Caitlin Lythgoe (8) 122
Paul Fuller (10) 122
Hannah Spencer (8) 122
Joel Chapman (11) 123
Lewis Kirby (8) 123
John Hearfield (8) 123

Wellesbourne School, Norris Green
Amy Evans (10) 124
Jack Hodgkinson (10) 124
Nathan Goldby (10) 125
Loni Crossland (10) 125
Francesca Davies (10) 126
Lisa Roberts (10) 127
Georgina Jarrold (11) 128
Kyle Hesketh (10) 129
Ashley Chiocchi (10) 130
Joe Chiocchi (10) 131
Lauren Fox (10) 132
Alisha Roberts (11) 133
Stephen McKee (10) 134
Matthew Provost (10) 135
Natasha Wright (10) 136
Steven Lambert (10) 137
Alex Walker (10) 138
Kyle Newby (10) 139
Gemma Bishop (11) 140
Jake Riley (10) 141
Laura Gladwinfield (10) 142
Laura Teare (10) 143
Jordan Lamb (10) 144
Wesley Cave (10) 145

Woodlands Primary School, Birkenhead
   Danielle Jamieson (11)   145
   Lindsay Watson (10)   146
   Masuma Begum (10)   146
   Nicole Hartley (10)   147

The Poems

I Wake Today

I wake today,
Get out of bed,
Then stretch and yawn
And scratch my head.

I find my clothes
I pull them on
While stifling
Another yawn.

I grab a breakfast
Bar for fuel
And hoist my pack
And head to school.

When I arrive
I'm truly shocked.
The lights are off,
The door is locked.

I check my watch
It's me, not them
I overslept.
It's 4pm.

Anya Gillin (10)
Arnot Community School, Liverpool

An Acrostic Poem

H is for harvest when we celebrate what we have got.
A is for autumn when the leaves on the trees fall.
R is for rainbows that brighten up the skies.
V is for vegetables which the farmers grow.
E is for the estuaries where the rivers flow
S is for the sunshine that we need to make the crops and
                                    flowers grow.
T is for trees that blow in the wind.

Megan Cavanagh (10)
Arnot Community School, Liverpool

Mrs Foulkes

Mrs Foulkes is the best
So much better than the rest.

Mrs Foulkes is very kind to me
She fills my day with joy and glee.

Mrs Foulkes is very funny
She has lots of money.

Mrs Foulkes' scones are great
And I couldn't have picked a better mate.

Mrs Foulkes is very kind
And she has a good mind.

This is my poem about Mrs Foulkes,
She makes a lovely pan of scouse
And when her day is over and gone
She has a cup of tea and a home-made scone!

Kayla Thompson (9)
Arnot Community School, Liverpool

Kennings Dog

Cat catcher
Tail wagger
Meat eater
Light sleeper
Eye weeper
Milk licker
Pigeon hater
Inpatient waiter
Basket sleeper
Good entertainer.

Ryan Landry (10)
Arnot Community School, Liverpool

Kennings Dogs

Tail wagger
Meat eater
Dog barker
Silent sleeper
Dog howler
Night creeper
Bone digger
Night sleeper.

Nikita Aspinwall (10)
Arnot Community School, Liverpool

My Riddle

Everyone has one
It begins with an 'f'
They play together
I am part of one
Everyone is one
Mine is never gone
They're always there for each other
We respect it
What is it?
Family.

Rebecca Sealeaf (9)
Arnot Community School, Liverpool

Allo Allo

P icking up the bad guys
O r trying to stop crime
L ooking out for car thieves
I n the middle of the night
C aring for the community
E veryone young and old.

Daniel Melia (10)
Arnot Community School, Liverpool

Football

I like to play football it is great
I enjoy playing it with my mates

Whether it's at play or at dinner time
I respect my friends because they are kind

Every match day I just can't wait to see
Liverpool my team; the best of best can be

The player I admire an awful lot
Is Cisse, without him we go to pot

I respect the job they do and the fact that they are my team
I admire, honour, value and regard as they are the best I've ever seen.

Mark James (9)
Arnot Community School, Liverpool

My Goldfish

I have two little goldfish
Their names are Jack and Jill
But at the moment I am really sad because one of them is ill

You are probably thinking, 'What's this all about?'
I'll tell you now so listen, promise not to shout

My fish are just two creatures I value with my heart
Although they cannot talk to you it would be sad if we were apart

I'm going to end this poem now
But just remember this
Things don't have to talk or listen to you,
To respect and dearly miss.

Billiejo Fairclough (10)
Arnot Community School, Liverpool

Dinner Time

Our dinner lady has come
Fish fingers, beans, dessert
Yum-yum.
I sit on my table with my friends
Every bit of dinner is good for my tum.

I wonder what I'm having for dinner
Sit up nicely and we can go
Gab, gab, gab
I tell them to shush
Now we're last now and they say, 'so'.

Finally we're going for our dinner
Oohh, ham, chips and peas
I hope I'm in time to get extras
All this food is just for me.

Debra Bell (9)
Arnot Community School, Liverpool

Britney Spears

Britney Spears is the best
Better than all the rest

She is my favourite popstar
Inspirational is what you are

I really like her songs
No matter what she does wrong

I'm not sure my mum will agree
But I can have my opinions, they are free.

Ashleigh Buckley (9)
Arnot Community School, Liverpool

Sunny Dinner Times

At dinner time we go out and play
Years 3 and 4 eat their dinner first
So Years 5 and 6 go away and play games
And children are so happy they laugh like they will burst

And now the Years 3 and 4 are out
We can go in and have our dinner
When we get in the hall the lady will ring the bell
And it's time to go back to class and I look a bit thinner.

Katie Lau (10)
Arnot Community School, Liverpool

Playtimes

Coats, hats, scarves and gloves
So we don't get a cold
Down the stairs, where's that racket?
'I found them Miss,' they'll get told!

Now we're outside in the tuck queue
And that cold is running down my spine
Playtime is over, finishing our crisps
All stand still and get into your line.

Abbie Davies (9)
Arnot Community School, Liverpool

Fun

Fun is pink, like when you blush
To me fun sounds like people laughing cheerfully
Fun tastes like cold, melting ice cream
Fun looks like a pink rose
Fun feels like the sand on the beach
Fun smells like a bright red flower.

Jenna Potter (8)
Blacklow Brow Primary School, Huyton

The Riverside

As the river bounced side to side
It pushed its debris where the water rats hide
The river found another route
And on a rock the man play the flute
In the river the fish hide
From the seagulls that glide
Lurking around for their prey
They watch, listening all day
Until they catch something at
The end of the day.

Sean Givnan (10)
Blacklow Brow Primary School, Huyton

River Digondo

The clouds were heavy
And dropped their babies
The rain hit the mountain
And ran down into the river
And skipped away quickly
The river went round a meander
And met someone called Leander.

Kyle Limbert (11)
Blacklow Brow Primary School, Huyton

Silence

Silence is white like a melting snowman
Silence sounds like people whispering in class
Silence tastes like salt in a bottle of orange juice
Silence looks like the light blue sky and the puffy clouds
Silence feels like a mall that has nothing in it
Silence smells like my best friend's house
Silence reminds me of me, my friends and school.

Luke Birchall (8)
Blacklow Brow Primary School, Huyton

The River's Journey

As the river came around the meander, it
Threw the rocks aside.
It also stole some earth, as it twisted
Around the outside.
The rocks skipped down the river
They seemed to be having a race.
It was going far too fast, it missed a
Bend which made an oxbow lake
Two rivers ran to meet to form a tributary
Just before they slipped and fell into the sea
The journey was not over yet, as the sun dragged
The water droplets to the sky.
Then they parachuted down again
To form a river that would never die.

Stephanie Weston (10)
Blacklow Brow Primary School, Huyton

The River Dance

Down the mountain the water flows
In and out the watery grove
As the water flew down the hill
Smoothly, gently like a graceful windmill.

But violently bashing the helpless rocks
Carrying them away as if they're light as socks
But dropping them off here and there
They're scattered around almost everywhere.

Around the meander, then the oxbow
Down the tributary, off we go
Enter the sea, freedom again
But only to share the agonising pain!

Liam Lannigan (11)
Blacklow Brow Primary School, Huyton

A River Poem

The tributary followed
The slow, smooth water into the river
The water went very quickly around all the bends
The waves turned around the meander
While it crumpled into little pieces
While the rocks were still
They watched the waves rushing past
The waves were loud and quick as
They zoomed past every rock and bend
The huge oxbow lake curled around
The deep blue river.
The end of the river waited impatiently
While the oxbow lake frowned
The waves finally ended
And met with the sea.

Jazmine Moody (10)
Blacklow Brow Primary School, Huyton

Around The River

The rocks swim in the lake
The river screams it is in a state
That's not all, the boulders attack
But luckily, it could deposit and come back
Around the river the trees stare
The river isn't all that bare
It can be bright, it can be dull
It can be empty, it can be full
This river is a nice place to be
And there is a lot of nature to see.

Louis Weston (10)
Blacklow Brow Primary School, Huyton

The Runaway River

The river is running faster
Than lightning
But what from?

The river throws the rocks to
The side and picks up the mud
Beneath as it passes.

The river is running faster
Than lightning
But what from?

The river eats away the earth
And pushes some to the side.

The river is running faster
Than lightning
But what from?
But what from?
But what from?

Laura Gilmore (10)
Blacklow Brow Primary School, Huyton

The Key To The Sea

As the stones swam across the river,
The rocks on the bank started to quiver
One by one the rocks jumped off
Onto the ruffled river cloth.

As the mountain nears and nears
The water changes its gears
Now the rocks have reached the fast part
Side to side the rocks dart.

Now the water has found the key
To the bigger thing, the sea!

Stephanie McVey (10)
Blacklow Brow Primary School, Huyton

Whirlpool

The river bullied some small, innocent rocks into the side of the river
During a heavy rainfall, the river punched the rocks
Eroding into tiny pieces, smaller than the first hand of a clock
The cloud spilled a cup of water
And as the river started to flow on flatter land
The water in the river started to saunter
It even started to deposit some sand
The river cheated in a race by cutting through a meander creating an oxbow lake
And it sliced and diced some pebbles like they were one big cake.

Sophie Gaffney (10)
Blacklow Brow Primary School, Huyton

The River's Rapids

The river's rapids are as fast as lightning
Sometimes it can get frightening
The water hits the rocks and makes a splash
It really looks like one big crash
When the water begins to fall
With the spray, you cannot see at all
As it hits the rocks below
That is what makes the river flow.

Jonathan Daly (10)
Blacklow Brow Primary School, Huyton

Silence

Silence is white like white fluffy clouds
Silence sounds like nothing when someone is upset
Silence tastes like bacon warm in a pan
Silence feels like a cotton wool ball all fluffy, woolly and warm
Silence looks like clouds in the light blue sky
Silence smells like egg in a pan all warm and nice
Silence reminds me of a day on the hill, all quiet and nice.

Emma Clarke (8)
Blacklow Brow Primary School, Huyton

Silence

Silence is the colour of white, like white puffy clouds in the sky
Silence sounds like the snow falling out of the sky
Silence tastes like cold water in my mouth
Silence smells like the wind gently blowing
Silence looks like stars in the sky at night
Silence feels like a melted snowman
It reminds me of the clouds in the sky on a winter's day.

Megan Roper (9)
Blacklow Brow Primary School, Huyton

Fear

Fear is grey like clouds getting ready to thunder
Fear sounds like thunder
Fear tastes like thunder going down my throat
Fear smells like terrible thunder going down to the floor
Fear looks like sharp devil forks
Fear feels like thunder going to hit me.

Millie Weston (8)
Blacklow Brow Primary School, Huyton

Fear Poem

Fear is grey like a thunderstorm
Fear sounds like shouting
Fear tastes like I have just eaten a lemon
It smells like fire
It looks like a fist
It feels all hard
It reminds me of getting bullied.

Ellie Wallace (9)
Blacklow Brow Primary School, Huyton

A Happiness Poem

Happiness is yellow and jolly
Happiness sounds like jolly things
Happiness tastes like soft ice cream
It smells like a lovely, jolly smell
It looks like funny things
It feels soft and cuddly
It reminds me of when I went to the funfair
I was so happy.

James Shone (8)
Blacklow Brow Primary School, Huyton

Fear Is . . .

Fear is orange like the sun, will never go down
Fear sounds like clouds crashing with thunder
Fear tastes like sweet and sour bits in my mouth
Fear looks like dull clouds getting ready to thunder
Fear feels like snow melting in my hands
Fear smells like smoke burning in the distance
Fear reminds me of my grandad dying.

Hope Whewell (8)
Blacklow Brow Primary School, Huyton

Fun

Fun is pink, a bit like boiled ham
Fun sounds like children picking rosy-pink roses
Fun tastes like children licking an ice lolly
Fun looks like people jumping as high as a bird
Fun smells like a lovely summer day.

Brittany Heyes (8)
Blacklow Brow Primary School, Huyton

Jump And Jiggle

Rhinos charge, hippos barge
Cats pounce, kangaroos bounce
Ferrets bite, tigers fight
Sea lions clap, crocs snap
Snakes slither, chimps shiver
Rabbits squeak, squirrels peek
Mice small, giraffes tall
Elephants fat, birds chat
But I walk and talk.

Simon Ridgway (9)
Blacklow Brow Primary School, Huyton

Fun

The colour of fun to me is baby-blue like raindrops
Fun sounds like little children splashing in puddles
Fun tastes to me like ice crackling in a glass
Fun looks like children jumping on a big trampoline
Fun feels like my first time walking on the sand
Fun smells like the salty sea.

Abbie Wood (8)
Blacklow Brow Primary School, Huyton

Fun Poem

Fun is yellow like the sun
Fun to me sounds like cheering
Fun to me is like ice cream
To me fun looks like a sunny day
Fun feels like sand running through my hands on the beach.

Ruth Peach (8)
Blacklow Brow Primary School, Huyton

Volcano, Volcano

Volcano, volcano is so red and so hot
I wouldn't like to do anything for it
Or you will have to do a lot.

Volcano, volcano please will you stop
Otherwise I will also get so hot.

Volcano, volcano if you don't stop
I will have to throw you in the hot pot.

Abbie McCormack (9)
Blacklow Brow Primary School, Huyton

Fear Is . . .

Fear is black like my black cat
Fear sounds like the hurricanes are coming
Fear tastes like a rotten apple, sweet and sour
Fear smells like a power plant burning down
Fear looks like the sun has disappeared
Fear feels like the rain is drifting away in my hands
Fear reminds me of the days when the rain falls down.

Naomi Birbeck (8)
Blacklow Brow Primary School, Huyton

Sadness

Sadness is blue like the ocean
Sadness sounds like a bird in a tree
Sadness looks dull
Sadness smells like mud
Sadness feels like a rainy day.

Russell Taylor (8)
Blacklow Brow Primary School, Huyton

Her Name Was Mary

Her name was Mary
She lived down the road
Everyone says she is a ghost
But I don't believe them
I say she is a witch
I have seen her broomstick
I go past her house
Every day to go to school
I have had a sleepover at her house
I saw her broomstick in her wardrobe
When I asked her, she said, 'No'
And quickly shut the wardrobe door.

Jessica Harvey (9)
Blacklow Brow Primary School, Huyton

Love

Love is red like a flashing heart
Love is like a beat of a heart
Love is like a sweet strawberry
Love is like the smell of petals
Love looks like a bird in the sky
Love feels like a teddy bear.

Heidi Ridgway (7)
Blacklow Brow Primary School, Huyton

Sadness

Sadness is the colour grey like a big grey cloud
Sadness sounds like tears exploding where they fall
Sadness tastes bitter like lemons in a jar
Sadness smells like old socks
Sadness looks like an old junkyard
Sadness feels like a thunderstorm.

Charlie Vidamour (7)
Blacklow Brow Primary School, Huyton

A Tropical Storm

Boats smashed at sea
Masts torn
Raging winds, G-force three or four
Battering rain
Almost no heat
People being swept off their feet
Roofs torn off houses
People screaming, off washing lines fly trousers
No electricity, none at all
Over goes a weak brick wall
All because of a tropical storm.

Daniel Turnley (9)
Blacklow Brow Primary School, Huyton

A Happy Day

Happy is the colour yellow
Happy birds tweeting in the sky
Happy like a juicy apple on a tree
Happy like the air conditioning from the car
Happy like flowers dropping from the sky
Happy is soft, like a pillow.

Lewis Cox (7)
Blacklow Brow Primary School, Huyton

Darkness

Darkness is the colour black, like a big midnight cat
Darkness sounds like the wings of a bat
Darkness tastes freezing cold, like the ice sea
Darkness smells like a dusty closet
Darkness looks like a pitch-black night
Darkness feels scary like a big, hairy monster.

Patrik Taylor (7)
Blacklow Brow Primary School, Huyton

Monsters

Monsters are big, little and medium
Monsters can be purple or green
Monsters smell like sewer pipes
Monsters don't taste like anything
Monsters are ugly and horrible
Monsters feel gooey and slimy.

Stephanie Wood (7)
Blacklow Brow Primary School, Huyton

Love

Love is the colour red, like big lovely hearts
Love sounds silent like when you're hugging pets
Love tastes like big, crunchy toast
Love smells like flowers in the fresh air
Love looks like a field with the smell of corn
Love feels like fresh violets.

Jamie White (7)
Blacklow Brow Primary School, Huyton

Darkness

Darkness is the colour black, like a midnight cat
Darkness tastes cold like the really cold air
Darkness feels scary like big, black, scary monsters
Darkness smells horrible like big, black armpits
Darkness looks like a really dark mouth
Darkness sounds like bats' wings.

Matthew Morris (7)
Blacklow Brow Primary School, Huyton

Happiness

Happiness is the colour yellow, like a big yellow sun
Happiness sounds like the birds singing
Happiness tastes like the morning breeze
Happiness smells like chips, fresh out of the oven
Happiness looks like flowers in a meadow
Happiness feels like joy and laughter.

Catherine Arnold (7)
Blacklow Brow Primary School, Huyton

Love

Love is the colour of lovely light red
Love is the sound of a little star sparkling
Love is the taste of delicious pizza
Love smells like sausages fresh from the oven
Love is like a volcano bursting into flames
Love feels like you love your pet so much.

Callum Reardon (7)
Blacklow Brow Primary School, Huyton

Anger

Anger is the colour red, like a shining, bright ruby
Anger sounds quiet, like a deserted, haunted house
Anger tastes hot, like boiling, roast potatoes
Anger smells boiling, like a big, raging fire
Anger looks red, like a big, exploding volcano
Anger feels hard, like a big, hard wall.

David Murphy (7)
Blacklow Brow Primary School, Huyton

Happiness

Happiness is the colour blue like the big, blue ocean
Happiness sounds loud like a happy family
Happiness tastes warm like sweet hot chocolate
Happiness smells clean like a big, new house
Happiness looks bright like the big, hot sun
Happiness feels kind like a helpful human.

Haaris Moynihan (8)
Blacklow Brow Primary School, Huyton

Darkness

Darkness is the colour black, like a midnight bat
Darkness sounds silent, like the roaring of a werewolf
Darkness tastes like the cold wind
Darkness smells like cobwebs
Darkness looks like a scary, black forest
Darkness feels like a big monster.

Matthew Thomalla (7)
Blacklow Brow Primary School, Huyton

Happiness

Happiness is the colour of a big bunch of flowers
Happiness is the sound of a happy flutter of the wind
Happiness tastes like a big bunch of candyfloss
Happiness smells like a sweet shop with candyfloss in
Happiness looks like a lovely bowl of happy thoughts
Happiness feels like a lovely hug from my family.

Mollie Christopher (7)
Blacklow Brow Primary School, Huyton

Darkness

Darkness is a slimy mud puddle
Darkness is a wolf howling at midnight
Darkness tastes like a freezing cold glass of ice-cold water
Darkness smells of chips baking in the oven
Darkness looks like a cape covering half of the world
Darkness feels like a shadow is following me.

Olivia Rose Hood (7)
Blacklow Brow Primary School, Huyton

Fear

Fear is the colour blue like a cold windy day
Fear sounds loud like a monster killing a city
Fear tastes cold like the North Pole
Fear smells of garlic, like a garlic dump
Fear looks like a little blue elf
Fear feels like you want to hide in a corner and never come out.

Rachel Benbow (8)
Blacklow Brow Primary School, Huyton

Love

Love is red like a red petal on a rose
Love is like the sound of a kiss
Love is like the taste of lipstick
Love is like the smell of a rose
Love is like a bird flying in the sky
Love feels hot.

Chloe Webster (7)
Blacklow Brow Primary School, Huyton

What Would I Be?

If I were something to do with a forest
What would I be?
Would I be a small plant or a tall tree?

If I were something to do with the sea
Where would I live?
Would I live in a big cave or a place so small it could get
through a sieve?

If I were something to do with animals
What would I be?
Would I be a slow turtle or something as crafty as a bee?

If I were something to do with the desert
What would I eat?
Would I eat plants or search and eat meat?

If I were something to do with Earth
What would I be?
Would I be someone else, or would I be *me*?

Maria Blanchflower (9)
Blacklow Brow Primary School, Huyton

Darkness

Darkness is the colour black, like a big mighty cat
Darkness sounds loud like the heavy flaps of a bat
Darkness tastes cold, like the wind on my lips
Darkness smells dusty, like smelly toilets that are out of order
Darkness looks like a big, black, scary cave
Darkness feels scary, like a big, black and purple monster.

Alexandra Weston (8)
Blacklow Brow Primary School, Huyton

A Bird In The Haunted House

I walked down the
path very
scared
I opened the
door and
there was
a
bird.

The bird was so
big he
flapped
like a
bee
and now
he lives at home
with me!

Matthew Donnelly (9)
Blacklow Brow Primary School, Huyton

Jump And Jiggle

Seals clap
Crocodiles snap
Babies cry
Birds fly
Caterpillars hump
Frogs jump
Lions prowl
Werewolves howl.

Ross Swift (9)
Blacklow Brow Primary School, Huyton

On The Beach

Whoosh, whoosh, whoosh
The sound of the water crashing against the rock
The waves hitting the seagulls
The sound of music
The smell of hot dogs and chips
You can see sandcastles in the distance
Children playing in the sand and in the water
Playing ball games
People sunbathing on deckchairs
And children getting ice cream
And children picking shells and putting them in buckets
Flowers blowing in the wind from side to side.

Philippa Gee (9)
Blacklow Brow Primary School, Huyton

Volcano, Volcano

Volcano, volcano
I love you a lot
You shoot up so tall
And fall so wide
With luminous colours you go into the sky.

Emma Gibson (9)
Blacklow Brow Primary School, Huyton

Volcano!

We saw a volcano
Up so high
We went to the top
And I wondered why
It started to cough and splutter its flame
I looked at my friend and he was to blame
Run!

Daniel Daly (9)
Blacklow Brow Primary School, Huyton

Tornadoes

Tornadoes spin around and round
As it spins they pick up anything on the ground
They can even pick up bins off the ground
They are so strong that they go round
So strong they can pick up anything!
They can kill!

Alex Gynane (9)
Blacklow Brow Primary School, Huyton

The Forest

In the forest
Cold at night
Wolves howling
In the distance
Footsteps, I
Run as fast as
I can.

Daniel Dacey (9)
Blacklow Brow Primary School, Huyton

The Sky!

The sky is blue
The sky is bright
All the birds fly out at night
I wish I could be one of them
And fly away home!

Katie Mahoney (9)
Blacklow Brow Primary School, Huyton

Love

Love is pink, like warm food in my belly
   It sounds like peace and quiet
      It tastes like soft sweets
         It smells like a nice rose
           It looks like love hearts
              It feels like soft cushions
                 It reminds me of McDonald's nuggets and fries.

Cerys Edden (9)
Carr Mill Primary School, St Helens

Colour

Green is like wind blowing trees on a windy day
Red is like danger when a bull is charging at you
Purple is like thunder crashing down to the Earth
Yellow is like the sun shining on a summer's day
Blue is like the waves crashing on the rocks at the seaside
White is like snow floating down to the ground.

Kirsty Clayton (9)
Carr Mill Primary School, St Helens

Love

Love is like a feather pillow
It sounds like a bird singing
It tastes like a creamy, soft toffee
It smells like a bunch of flowers
Love looks like the glistening stars
Love feels great
Love reminds me of a smile when I have helped someone.

Robert Smith Latham (9)
Carr Mill Primary School, St Helens

Anger

Anger is red like the sun
With boiling flames
It sounds like babies crying
It tastes lie sour lemons
It smells like all the fresh
Trees in the woods
It looks like the sky
When it thunders
It feels like sloppy mud
It reminds me of hitting people.

Linda Lee (9)
Carr Mill Primary School, St Helens

Anger

Anger is black, like darkness
It sounds like a howling wolf
It tastes like a mouldy mud pie
It smells like the city dump
It looks like a black devil's shadow
It feels like creepy, crawling spiders
It reminds me of home alone loneliness.

Jessica Masters (9)
Carr Mill Primary School, St Helens

Anger

Anger is red like an erupting volcano
It sounds like my sister calling me
It tastes like sour milk
It smells like petrol
It looks like a full board of work!
It feels like war.

Darren Thelwell (9)
Carr Mill Primary School, St Helens

Anger!

Anger is grey, like clouds falling in on you
It sounds like electricity exploding
Its taste is sour, like a lemon fizzing up in my mouth
It smells like sour milk that has been left on the window sill
Anger looks like a dark, cold room with shadows moving around you
Anger feels like you're falling into a bush with thorns sticking into you
Anger reminds me of people suffering that have done nothing wrong.

Samantha Pye (9)
Carr Mill Primary School, St Helens

Happy

Happiness is yellow like the lovely sun
It sounds like children's laughter
It tastes like a nice lemon
It smells like someone's breath when they've brushed their teeth
Happiness feels like a smooth teddy bear
Happiness looks like a sunflower growing
It reminds me of going on holiday to Puerto Rico.

Jordan Hale (9)
Carr Mill Primary School, St Helens

Anger

Anger is black like the shadows of darkness
It sounds like cracking and shaking bones
It tastes like red-hot chilli peppers
It smells like a toilet, that has not been flushed
It feels like a mouldy worm cake
It reminds me of dark times.

Robert Lever (9)
Carr Mill Primary School, St Helens

Happiness

Happiness is yellow, like a hot, shining sun
It sounds like children playing and laughing
It tastes like a big chocolate cake that's just been made
Happiness feels like a soft, silk pillow when you snuggle down in it
Happiness reminds me of a hot summer holiday when you go
                                                   to the beach.

Marissa Donnellan (9)
Carr Mill Primary School, St Helens

Happiness

Happiness is red, like a rose in a flower bed
It sounds like a soft wind
It tastes like a piece of chocolate
It looks like a person smiling
Happiness feels like you have loads of friends
Happiness reminds me of butterflies.

Katrina Hilton (9)
Carr Mill Primary School, St Helens

Happiness

Happiness is green like the softness of nature
It tastes like a piece of Galaxy
It smells like my mum's perfume
Happiness looks like a cute cat
Happiness feels like a big teddy
Happiness reminds me of my sister.

Kieron Dixon (9)
Carr Mill Primary School, St Helens

Sadness

Sadness is black like an angry panther
It sounds like a pounding roar going around my head
Sadness tastes like chewy pork meat
When you want to get something better on the plate
It smells like a man who lives on the street and has not had a bath
It looks like a dead flower with all the petals falling off
Sadness is when I get tormented on the playground
Sadness reminds me of when I lost my best toy in the
                                      whole wide world.

Callum Gray (9)
Carr Mill Primary School, St Helens

Blue Is . . .

The sky is blue,
Blue is the colour of a dragonfly with lace wings
Blue is the colour of the deepest sea
Blue is the colour of the dolphin jumping with glee!

Kieran Cunningham (10)
Clifford Holroyde Centre of Expertise, Liverpool

Anger

Anger is a volcano erupting
A fireball inside you
Waiting to come out
Anger is stamping your feet
Slamming your desk
That is anger.

Katrina Burns (9)
Higher Bebington Junior School, Wirral

What Is Water?

Water is still
Water is calm
Water is something you can't harm
Water helps boats sail and sail
Water helps different whales
Water helps trees
Water helps bees
Water helps you live and live
That's what water can give.

Abbi Penketh (9)
Higher Bebington Junior School, Wirral

Friends

Friends are there when you need them
Friends show they care
Friends make us smile
Friends make us sad
But me I am very glad
That I have my *friends*.

Jamie-Lee Sadler (10)
Higher Bebington Junior School, Wirral

Snowflakes

Snowflakes float through the air
They shine and glitter like diamonds
They are soft and cold, but me
I am bold and build a great big snowman
When I am done, I show my mum
Who gives me a big mug of cocoa.

Emma Sadler (7)
Higher Bebington Junior School, Wirral

Our Molly

Our Molly comes from far away
We went to get her one sunny day
She's chocolate-brown with ears to the ground
A nose to sniff and a tail to stiff
Molly chews and chews, take care of your shoes
She comes from Sussex, way down south
Has a brother in Spain and a sister in Denmark
She's very quick off the mark
She is nine months old and does not do as she is told
She has eaten two TV remote controls
And shows no sign of the remotest control
She is a rare breed and hard to feed
But what she does like
Is smelly old tripe.

Matthew Herbison (7)
Higher Bebington Junior School, Wirral

Bath Time

Turn on the water
Not too hot
Pour in the bubble stuff
In goes the lot.

In goes my duck
In goes my boat
In goes all the things
That I can float.

Now my bath is ready
What else can there be?
Oh, I think I remember,
In goes me!

Calista Dufton-Kelly (10)
Higher Bebington Junior School, Wirral

The Noisy Jungle

There's a party in the jungle
With animals far and wide
Party hats and party cakes
What a big surprise!

The monkeys jumping,
The hippos bumping,
The lions roaring,
The gorilla thumping.

The rhinos dancing,
The giraffes so tall
And the elephants
Playing basketball.

So there's a party in the jungle
With animals far and wide
Party hats and party cakes
What a big surprise!

George Anderson (8)
Higher Bebington Junior School, Wirral

Jolly Jilly

Jolly Jilly jumps so high
Up she goes like a fly
Little Jilly jogs about
Watching people catching trout.

Lovely little Jilly goes to bed
And on her pillow
Lies her head.

Niamh Meehan (7)
Higher Bebington Junior School, Wirral

Sisters

My two sisters are like cat and dog
Sometimes I call them both a warthog
One sister can be a pain
But two sisters drive me insane!

Emma always takes my stuff
But now she's taken more than enough
Paper, books, pens and more
Until she makes me lock my door.

Laura sometimes can be fun
But when Matt rings, she's off to run
Up to her bedroom to catch the call
And then she's no fun at all.

Emma's bad, but can be nice
She's helped me out, once or twice
She makes me giggle, laugh and smile
Once with her I walked a mile!

Laura's fine, she's quite divine
One night she took me out to dine
She does my hair and toenails blue
She would like my hair to be straight too.

Sisters really aren't too bad
And sometimes I'm really quite glad
If they were worse I'd cut my hair
Until I screamed, because it was bare!

Jenny Cook (10)
Higher Bebington Junior School, Wirral

The 11+

The 11+ is hard and cruel
But if you work hard
You'll get a great school.

There are lots of schools
To apply for
Like Wirral and Beb High.

As long
As you work at your best
You'll be an angel in the sky.

Our head teacher helps us
To be an 11+ swot
But when he suggests the methods
We all think, *what, what, what?*

As long
As you work your best
And always try
You'll soon be an 11+ angel in the sky.

Eleanor Meehan (10)
Higher Bebington Junior School, Wirral

Sunset

As day turns into night
An orange colour fills the sky
Here I watch till midnight as the sun sets in the east.

Orange, yellow, red, gold and tan
Fill this land with happiness and joy
Suns north, east, south, west
Need to rest.

The last light brings
Warmth and hope for another day
Tonight is a beautiful sunset!

Rachel Williams (11)
Higher Bebington Junior School, Wirral

The Soldier

In the distance he can see
Enemy lines of blue, green and red.
Mainly Scottish clansmen
Fighting for a prince.

The soldier sharpens his sword
Starts to load his gun.
He clips a bayonet on the end
And looks at the enemy.

The order to fire comes after a minute
Red coats cock their guns . . .
And fire - the nearest enemy fall!
The soldier reloads and fires again.

The enemy is retreating!
The soldier's army has won!
Back to camp the soldiers march
Although tired, everyone is smiling.

Victory!
Extra rum all round!
Extra pay and promotion!
Some things about being a soldier weren't that bad!

Ben Savage (8)
Higher Bebington Junior School, Wirral

Fire

Fire is like a lion in a cage,
Roaring and mean
Fire is like a runner,
Burning and hot
Fire tastes like red-hot chilli peppers
Fire has an indigo flame,
Burning for evermore.

Sarah Taylor (10)
Higher Bebington Junior School, Wirral

Victorian Children

The children long ago didn't live as long as we
And when I went to Wigan Pier, this is what I could see.

There were children working down the mine, in the factory and the mill
The working conditions were horrendous and often they felt ill.

They didn't have much money and nothing much to eat
But had to work all day long on their tiny little feet.

The rich were very lucky and got to go to school
But the school was strict and punishment was intensely cruel.

Kings and queens could change the way things were
But, for the poor, they didn't really care.

If I was asked to go back in time
I'd say, 'No thank you, my life is fine!'

Sean Cavanagh (10)
Higher Bebington Junior School, Wirral

My Special Dragon

My special dragon helps me do chores
Washing-up, cleaning windows, even sweeping floors
My special dragon sometimes helps me cook from a very special
cookery book.

My dragon's special as he's soft and loving too
My special dragon is the colour blue
My special dragon doesn't breath fire, nor eat meat
So when he's being kind to you I give him a special treat.

My special dragon is important to me
And one day . . . you'll see!

Haidee Booth (9) & Dayna Booth (7)
Higher Bebington Junior School, Wirral

Memories

A memory is special
And as strong as a rugged rock

A memory is a rainbow
Bursting with colour

A memory is an orange fire
Crackling on calm blue water

A memory is a salty tear
And a joyful smile

A memory lays in a golden box
At the back of your mind

Like a little puppy
Waiting to be walked.

      Never to be forgotten.

Jessica Crane (11)
Higher Bebington Junior School, Wirral

Anger

Your face goes red
Your tongue goes black
Your knuckles go white
And you are
A sorry sight

It makes you feel all hot inside
I hate everything in sight

In the calm after the storm
My boiling blood has gone

My heart stops pounding like a drum
The world - it feels alright again.

Alex Butler (9)
Higher Bebington Junior School, Wirral

My Dog Mac

Mac, my little white dog
Sleeps like a log
When he is asleep
He looks like fallen snow
He is a fluffy little woofy
I really love him so.

Jessica Morris (7)
Higher Bebington Junior School, Wirral

What Are Friends?

Friends are like balloons
Once you let them go
You can never get them back

Friends are the ones who send
You a letter, fax or e-mail
During the summer holidays.

Friends are people who don't
Let you down, cheat you
Or snitch you out.

So grab a friend and put them to the test
I mean why not?

Charlotte Moore (9)
Higher Bebington Junior School, Wirral

The Sea

The sea is full of salt
It whirls and never halts

It's full of fish
That make a good dish

But sometimes they're eaten
By sharks!

Natalie Taylor (8)
Higher Bebington Junior School, Wirral

My Naughty Little Sister

I've got a sister and her name is Emma Lou
She threw my slipper down the loo

My naughty little sister bumped my head
And she had to go straight to bed

In school she never pays attention
And that is why she always gets detention.

My naughty little sister takes my toys
And when she plays she makes a lot of noise.

Paul Cavanagh (7)
Higher Bebington Junior School, Wirral

Happiness

She looks like bubbles floating through the fluffy clouds
She tastes like soft, bouncy, pink candyfloss won at a fair
She sounds like baby bluebirds cheeping sweetly
She smells like roses swaying calmly in the breeze
Happiness is everywhere.

Katrina Ryan (8)
Higher Bebington Junior School, Wirral

Happiness

Happiness is like a piece of cake
Munching in your mouth
Happiness is like playing a game
With your friends
Happiness is like happiness
Flowing through your body.

Daniel Siddorn (9)
Higher Bebington Junior School, Wirral

What Is A Book?

A book is . . .
A mind-numbing succession of endless words?
A dull file of tedious print?
A humdrum, wearisome, silent lecture.

No!

A book is . . .
A colourful land of new ideas,
A lively tale of complex emotions
A gripping journey with a surprise around every corner,
So many different worlds all rolled into one.

Underneath the dusty blue cover
Is a world of fantasy
Waiting to be explored
Inviting you to journey into worlds as yet unknown.

Jessie Evans (11)
Holy Trinity CE Primary School, Wirral

Autumn

Floating, frozen leaves falling from the sky,
And all the trees in autumn give a big sigh,
Hedgehogs getting curled ready for their sleep,
Big badgers going up the hills which are very steep,
Sneaky squirrels getting every nut they spy,
We're at home, all alone eating apple pie,
Whirling, winding winds going round madly,
Sometimes damaging things quite badly,
Fireworks crackling in the moonlight,
And bonfires crackling real loud all night,
Goodbye autumn, time to go,
Now autumn has gone, come winter,
Winter is coming,
Come, winter, come!
I will miss autumn a lot, a lot, a lot!

Jack Howse (7)
Holy Trinity CE Primary School, Wirral

Autumn

Bonfires burning slightly cold,
Freezing freezer frosty mould,
Golden leaves falling and gloomy skies,
All animals screaming cries.
Hedgehogs hibernating in hideout lairs,
Freezing lonely lakes and mines in pairs.
Summer happiness has gone,
Soundless, soundless, struggling swan,
Swirling, spinning, windy sky,
Sitting eating delicious apple pie,
Winter ice and falling leaves,
Hot, haunted, hooting house,
Sleeping, silent, snuffling mouse,
Chattering teeth, getting cold,
Freezing pools I have been told.
Fireworks flying everywhere,
Windy sky in despair,
Wind changing like roses swaying,
Children happily running, playing,
In the playground in woolly hats,
Cats a-curling on cosy mats,
Sky as black as the darkest mud,
Playing in the playground when the ball goes *thud*.

Autumn ending, say goodbye to all the dark dull sky.

Emily McIlroy (8)
Holy Trinity CE Primary School, Wirral

My Teacher

My teacher is the best
She's better than the rest.
She makes learning a joy,
She's definitely not a boy!
My teacher is called Miss Davies
And she is the ace-ist.

Hannah Colley (9)
Holy Trinity CE Primary School, Wirral

The Months Of The Year

January brings the rain,
And it's a very big pain.

February brings the storm,
And it doesn't let us have any corn.

March has lovely flowers,
And doesn't have any showers.

April brings us beautiful flowers,
And we never get horrible showers.

May brings us sweet little chicks,
And they have the most beautiful licks.

June brings us a big yellow sun,
And the children come out to have some fun.

July it's the end of school,
And then the children will be cruel.

August we have ice cream,
And the seaside is all clean.

September is the greatest month,
And we never ever punch.

October brings us lovely fruit,
And the rain is really cute.

In November the animals sleep,
And maybe the sheep.

December it is Christmas time,
And I don't think I like lime.

Ellie Davies (8)
Holy Trinity CE Primary School, Wirral

Just 'Plane' Mad

Planes are big,
Planes are small,
They don't scare me
Much at all.
Fast ones,
Slow ones,
Way up high,
Dancing routines in the sky.
Taking off,
Landing screeches,
Runways, ships,
Or off the beaches.
Can you tell
I'm mad on planes,
I even watch them
When it rains.
My big bro's
In the RAF
He works hard
And has a laugh.
Now you know
What I like best,
Why don't you put me to the test?

Bradley Done (11)
Holy Trinity CE Primary School, Wirral

Autumn

Trees, trees, crunchy, crackling leaves,
Red, gold and orange sheaves,
Here comes the harvest time,
And people drink wine.
Blasting winds are coming your way,
Rain will come another day.
Bonfires are blasting out,
As little children scream and shout.

Anna Turner (7)
Holy Trinity CE Primary School, Wirral

My Poem About The Day

I woke up from my bed,
And this is what I said,
'Oh why, why, why!
Why is it a boring day?'

I went downstairs
And ate some pears.
I said, 'Oh why, why, why!
Why is it a boring day?'

I sat on my couch,
And shouted out, 'Ouch.'
I said, 'Oh why, why, why!
Why is it a boring day?'

Later on in the day
It carried on grey.
I said, 'Oh why, why, why!
Why is it a boring day?'

I tied my shoes in a bow,
And peeped out my window,
And I shouted, 'Hooray! Hooray!
It's not a boring day.'

Joe Smith (10)
Holy Trinity CE Primary School, Wirral

Autumn

Trees, trees, frozen leaves,
Up, up in high trees.

The squirrels are given nuts to eat
The ground covered with an icy sheet.

The birds are flying south tonight,
The sunset glows very bright.

So now it's getting very late
So what's that creak in the gate?

Hannah Waddington (7)
Holy Trinity CE Primary School, Wirral

My Light

In a large, dark room,
With the only colours grey or black,
Stands a tall,
Proud candle ready to bloom.

The candle shines . . . on and on,
The grey turns to blue,
The black to crimson,
This light shall never end . . .

Then the blue fades,
Even the crimson,
But the candle keeps on glistening.

In this world of horror,
Of cruelty and mean,
We have the candle of goodness,
To keep the world a-beam.

Oscar Reddrop (10)
Holy Trinity CE Primary School, Wirral

Autumn

Golden leaves hang down from trees,
Dull clouds bustling in the breeze,
Freezing frost on the ground,
Cold children gather round and round,
Golden and red leaves fall down,
Small faces start to frown,
People dress in woolly hats,
Like curled up cats on mats,
Fires are switched on,
As quick as they are gone.

Jenna Lavelle (7)
Holy Trinity CE Primary School, Wirral

Being Afraid

I felt afraid when I went to Chamelot
I was seven.
I felt afraid when I went on the whirlwind
I was seven.
I felt afraid when I went on the upside down ride
I was four.
I felt afraid when I was looking down
I was five.
I felt afraid when I went on the water slide
I was five.
I felt afraid when I went on the ghost train
I was five.
I felt afraid when I went on the horse
I was four.
I felt afraid when my sister got lost
Everyone was looking for her.
I was three.

Megan Edge (8)
Holy Trinity CE Primary School, Wirral

Autumn

Trees, trees, robins singing like bees,
Red and orange rustling leaves,
Hibernating hedgehogs sleep like dead leaves,
That fell from trees.
Snow drifts down and down,
Big trees are all brown,
Flowers blooming with all their might,
Showing all their beautiful light,
Crackling, crunchy leaves on the ground,
All the light will be found.

Simon Dore (7)
Holy Trinity CE Primary School, Wirral

My Poem

I'm trying to think of a poem,
How hard can it be?
At this very moment,
I would rather be listening to my CD.

I could write about flowers,
Even the sea,
The springtime joy,
But which should it be?

The horses in the meadow,
The dolphins out at sea,
The grass swaying in the breeze,
But what should it be?

What I want for Christmas,
The honey from the bee,
The whistling of the kettle,
But still what should it be?

The flowers in my garden,
Even my family,
The roaring of a winter fire,
But which should it be?

A road without cars,
A jungle without monkeys,
A flower without petals,
How terrible these would be.

I'm still trying to think of a poem,
How hard can it be?
And at this very moment,
I am listening to my CD!

Emma Fairbanks (10)
Holy Trinity CE Primary School, Wirral

What Of Our Tomorrows?

A planet from our children
That's not ruined beyond compare,
No birds submerged in oil,
Gasping out for air.

Why are we so selfish?
Just thinking of today
When happiness from childhood
Can never fade away.

Our air is filled with gases,
From our cars we love so much,
But what of our tomorrows,
And the people that we love?

Today is all that matters,
Is the attitude we share.
Just throw away our rubbish
Without a single care!

Deodorants and hairsprays
Looking after us today,
Just forget about our planet,
And the damage and decay.

Just think about tomorrow
And what our actions bring,
Can we afford such selfishness,
And the suffering it will bring?

Maria Manley (10)
Holy Trinity CE Primary School, Wirral

I Felt Afraid

I felt afraid of scary films if monsters came out of the telly.
I was three.
I felt afraid when I went to the dentist, when I opened my mouth.
I was four.
I felt afraid when I went swimming as if I drown.
I was five.
I felt afraid when I went on a plane. I was scared of heights.
I was six.
I felt afraid when I got a puppy, it was coming up to me.
I was two.
I felt afraid when I saw a fish, it was swimming up to me.
I was four.
I felt afraid when I went on a fast ride, it was scary.
I was eight.

Chelsea Morris (8)
Holy Trinity CE Primary School, Wirral

The Snake

                    The snake slithers silently
                    Through the long grass

It sneaks slowly
Upon its prey.

                    Then it strikes swiftly

And slides smoothly off
For a long stretch
Of slumber.

Philip McIlroy (10)
Holy Trinity CE Primary School, Wirral

Bravery Is . . .

Bravery is . . .

Sleeping at your friend's house for the first time
And not being scared.

Getting your first ever injection and not screaming.

Eating mango for the first time
When it's slippy, sloppy in your mouth.

Having a nosebleed and not screaming at the top of
My voice in terror.

Seeing string for the first time
And thinking it was a snake and not hiding.

Standing at the top of the stairs for the first time
And not falling down.

Going to reception when none of my friends were there
And not crying and running back to my mum.

Going up on stage for my first ever time
And not running off.

Daisy Manning (8)
Holy Trinity CE Primary School, Wirral

I Want To Be . . .

I want to be a hippo,
Not a big giraffe!

I want to be a chimpanzee,
With a cheeky laugh!

I want to be a kangaroo,
Jumping through the grass.

I want to be a parrot
Flying over the tropical sea.

Kelly Sinnett (9)
Holy Trinity CE Primary School, Wirral

The Animal Book

I went to a library
To see what might interest me

Had a look
At an animal book
It made me quite inspired:

Read about a sparrowhawk
How it flew
And how it walked

Flicked the page to a peregrine
With its glinting black feathers
And its powerful wing.

Looked up to the clock
Oh boy! What a shock -

I should be at home.

Lorin Thompson (10)
Holy Trinity CE Primary School, Wirral

A Heart Of Gold

I would like to tell you about a horse I once knew,
He was black and beautiful and cuddly too.
Can you guess who?
He's lovely to ride
But he couldn't be a bride!
He's brilliant to groom
But he couldn't use a broom!
He's quite hard to control,
But his heart is made of gold.
    You guessed it! It's
        Black Beauty.

Olivia Burnie (9)
Holy Trinity CE Primary School, Wirral

Bravery Is . . .

Bravery is . . .
Playing somebody else's violin when it is big
And hard to hold.

Bravery is . . .
Lying in the dark when all the shadows are dancing.

Bravery is . . .
Getting a new pair of shoes because you meet a new person
At the shop.

Bravery is . . .
Going to the hospital when I had impetigo.

Bravery is . . .
Looking after my mum when she had cut her hand
On a pane of glass.

Bravery is . . .
Going to school for the first time when everything
Looks big and frightening.

Bravery is . . .
Meeting my best friend when we haven't been in touch.

Laura Burton (8)
Holy Trinity CE Primary School, Wirral

School, School, School

Sometimes boring, not exciting,
Sometimes brill, dead inviting.
Teachers shout, teachers roar,
Get thrown out, stand by the door.
Sometimes work is really light,
Sometimes it is hard.
Sometimes you'll get into fights,
With people on the yard.

Rosie Evans (9)
Holy Trinity CE Primary School, Wirral

I Love The Library

The library, so big and strong,
It has every book from flowers to pong.

You never know what's round the corner,
It might be exciting, it might be a yawner!

It might be a book on how to cook meat,
It might be a book on how to play chess and cheat!

No, I think I won't become a shopkeeper
I think I'll be a person who looks after libraries instead.

Now I'm getting tired, it's time for bed,
I'll be back tomorrow that's for sure,
Now it's time to rest my sleepy head.

Ben Fitzpatrick (9)
Holy Trinity CE Primary School, Wirral

The Library

The library's cool,
If you have nowhere to go.
You'll sure find an interesting book,
Or you can find a competition
You can enter and win,
Or maybe hide in a dustbin!
Can you see an interesting book?
Just take it to the counter,
And sure they will let you take it out.
Just join and you will never be bored.
Find a new book every time,
Bring your old ones back.
Now become anything you want,
You will have or might have read about it.

Erica Daley (9)
Holy Trinity CE Primary School, Wirral

Being Afraid

I felt afraid when I flew over New York
I was eight.

I felt afraid when a snake came towards me
I was seven.

I felt afraid when I read my story to Year 3
I was nine.

I felt afraid when I first swam
I was two.

I felt afraid when I first saw school
I was four.

I felt afraid when I first saw fire
I was three.

Oliver Jones (9)
Holy Trinity CE Primary School, Wirral

School

If work was banned,
I'd love it!

If break was banned,
I'd hate it!

If school was banned,
I'd love it!

But if friendship was banned,
I'd probably cry!

Chloe Trollone (9)
Holy Trinity CE Primary School, Wirral

Bravery Is . . .

Bravery is . . .

Going to the doctors to have an injection with a needle
that looks like a dagger.
Rushing to casualty out in a storm with my mum.
Admitting to my mum that I had broken the new telly.
Telling Dad I didn't do my homework when I knew he'd be angry.
Pretending not to be afraid of tweezers aiming for my foot.
Going up on stage and singing in front of lots of people
at New Year's Eve.
Reading out my story to my teacher when I have a frog in my throat.
Jumping in the deep end of the pool without armbands
for the first time.

Isobel Thierry-Simpson (9)
Holy Trinity CE Primary School, Wirral

I Felt Afraid

I felt afraid of scary dogs when they opened their mouths to bite
I was six.
I felt afraid of cackling witches zooming in the night
I was four.
I felt afraid of a boa constrictor sliding on the ground
I was eight.
I felt afraid of croaking frogs jumping up at me
I was two.
I felt afraid of Grandad's metronome tick-tocking furiously
I was three.

Alexandra Campbell (8)
Holy Trinity CE Primary School, Wirral

I Felt Afraid

I felt afraid of the BFG
When I had only just become three.

I felt afraid when knocking on my head teacher's door
When I was very nearly four.

I felt afraid when I looked at the sky,
But I was a big boy, I was five.

I felt afraid when I looked at earwigs,
But I was big, I was six!

Joel Thompson (8)
Holy Trinity CE Primary School, Wirral

Bravery Is . . .

Bravery is saying goodbye to my dad
Because he is going away for a month.
Bravery is going on a water log ride in Southport,
The ride was very, very high.
Bravery is being on a horse that looks like a mountain.
Bravery is being on a boat that takes ages to get to Ireland.
Bravery is my first time at a new school,
Because I don't know anyone.

Niamh Roberts (8)
Holy Trinity CE Primary School, Wirral

Bravery Is . . .

Bravery is climbing up the Eiffel Tower
When you think it's going to fall down.
Falling off a climbing frame and not crying.
Going to school the first time, and knowing nobody.
Growing up to be a teenager
When you don't want to be.

Nicola Alty (8)
Holy Trinity CE Primary School, Wirral

I Felt Afraid

I felt afraid when I went on a merry-go-round at the funfair
I was three.
I felt afraid when I was trying to get a spoon
Under a boiling hot pan
I was eight.
I felt afraid when I was getting my ears pierced
I was six.
I felt afraid when I went on the dragon ride
I was seven.

Kelly Manley (8)
Holy Trinity CE Primary School, Wirral

The Hurricane

The houses are blowing
The rain is snowing
The windows are glowing
The cars are gone
The hurricane is coming!
Run!

Jordan Gore (8)
Longton Lane Community Primary School, Rainhill

Red The Dog

Red is a star
He can run very far
He is cuddly and cute
He is such a beaut!
I'll love him to the end
Because he's my best friend.

Caitlin Hodgkinson (8)
Longton Lane Community Primary School, Rainhill

Autumn

Autumn leaves start falling from the trees
The weather's nice, a gentle breeze.
The moon's down early
Can't play out.
Tomorrow will be nice without a doubt.

Fiona Pye (8)
Longton Lane Community Primary School, Rainhill

My Goldfish

My goldfish
Doesn't do very much
He just swims and swims
Doesn't care anywhere
Hardly a bit
All he does is blow bubbles
That's the exciting bit
Just remember he's only a fish
My dad says he will batter him but
I say, *'No!'*

Alex Storey (8)
Longton Lane Community Primary School, Rainhill

Autumn

I can see fog in the air
I can smell smoke
I can feel smooth conkers
I can taste pumpkin pie.

Owen Briers (8)
Longton Lane Community Primary School, Rainhill

Animals

Butterflies are big
Butterflies are small
Butterflies are colourful
The best of all.

Cats are big
Cats are small
Cats chase rats
The worst of all.

Rabbits are big
Rabbits are small
Rabbits are fluffy
The best of all.

Frogs are big
Frogs are small
Frogs are slimy
The worst of all.

Hannah Morton (8)
Longton Lane Community Primary School, Rainhill

I Wonder What It's Like To Be An Animal

I wonder what it's like to be a rabbit,
Running all around,
Or maybe in the garden,
Digging in the ground.

I wonder what it's like to be a bird,
Flying in the sky,
Or maybe in a cage,
With someone by my side.

I wonder what it's like to be a fish,
Swimming in the sea,
Or maybe in a fish bowl,
With someone swimming with me.

Rhian Keating (8)
Longton Lane Community Primary School, Rainhill

Autumn

I like autumn
Autumn is fun
You get to play in the breeze
And jump in the leaves
Yes that's autumn.

I like autumn
Autumn is fun,
You get to play in with conkers
And be bonkers
Yes that's autumn.

I like autumn
Autumn is fun,
You get to play tricks
And pick up sticks
Yes that's autumn.

Erin Gray (8)
Longton Lane Community Primary School, Rainhill

My Cat

I love my cat
Cos it sits on a mat
And snuggles up to sleep
Without a peep.

I love my cat
Cos it miaows like that
And snuggles up to sleep
Without a peep.

I love my cat
Cos it chases that rat
And snuggles up to sleep
Without a peep.

Adam Prescott (8)
Longton Lane Community Primary School, Rainhill

I Wish, I Wish I Was A Fish

I wish, I wish I was a fish to swim through the deep blue sea.
I wish, I wish I was a fish to swim in the oceans free.
I would swim through the coral and swim through the reef,
                                        to see all the other fish.
I wish, I wish I was a fish to swim through the deep blue sea.

Daniel Vickers (8)
Longton Lane Community Primary School, Rainhill

Anger

Anger is red like a volcano
It sounds like an explosion
It tastes like chilli peppers
It smells like a fire burning
It feels like flames on your face
It looks like the Earth is cracking
It reminds me of a dog getting beaten up.

Adam Whitfield
Newton-le-Willows Primary School, Newton-le-Willows

Anger

Anger is red like a fire engine
It sounds like lightning on a pole
It tastes like rotten potatoes
It smells like gunge
It feels like red-hot coals
It reminds me of the nasty Devil.

Aarron Rae (10)
Newton-le-Willows Primary School, Newton-le-Willows

Anger

Anger is red, like a fierce dragon
It sounds like a tiger roaring
It tastes like a horrible medicine in my mouth
It smells like a fire burning inside me
It looks like a volcano exploding near me
It feels like a chilli burning on my hands
It reminds me of a war in Iraq.

Sasha Sandford
Newton-le-Willows Primary School, Newton-le-Willows

Anger

Anger is red like hot chilli peppers
It sounds like flames screaming
It tastes like a big hot curry
It smells like stinking potatoes
It looks like bubbling curry
It feels like red-hot coals
It reminds me of a witch's black cloak.

Lauren Bate
Newton-le-Willows Primary School, Newton-le-Willows

Anger

Anger is red, like a bursting volcano.
It sounds like a running fire engine.
It tastes like hot red strawberries.
It smells like rotten peppers.
It looks like red potatoes.
It feels like red apples.

Sophie Gregory (10)
Newton-le-Willows Primary School, Newton-le-Willows

Anger!

Anger is red, like a red angry devil
It sounds like stomping of feet in my head
It tastes like sour tomato juice
It smells like a smelly, rotten sewer
It looks like a red pepper
It feels like a lumpy whiteboard
It reminds me of a volcano erupting near me.

Jasmine Squires
Newton-le-Willows Primary School, Newton-le-Willows

Anger

Anger is red like a burning fire.
It sounds like a dog growling fiercely.
It tastes like chilli peppers.
It smells like a bonfire burning.
It looks like a volcano melting.
It feels like hot spicy curry.
It reminds me of an angry fox.

Laura Poultney
Newton-le-Willows Primary School, Newton-le-Willows

Anger

Anger is red like the sun's burning fire
It sounds like an explosion destroying electric wires
It smells like oil starting to set fire
It looks like a tiger catching its prey
It feels like a wasp stinging your arm
And it reminds me of a nuclear bomb strike on New York.

Perry Brockley
Newton-le-Willows Primary School, Newton-le-Willows

Anger

Anger is dull red like a volcano exploding.
It sounds like a storm.
It tastes like an apple that's gone mouldy.
It smells like fire burning.
It looks like red, dull smoke.
It feels warm.
It reminds me of rain.

Lauren Walsh
Newton-le-Willows Primary School, Newton-le-Willows

Anger!

Anger is black, like someone's fierce eyes.
It sounds like a tambourine giving you a banging headache.
It tastes like a burnt sausage.
It smells like rotten eggs.
It looks like mixed puddings.
It feels like a flame in a fire.

Alison Wood
Newton-le-Willows Primary School, Newton-le-Willows

Fear

Fear looks like flames of a fire.
It sounds like my shivering breath coming from my mouth.
It smells like my cold skin.
It feels like a cold hand on my shoulder.
Fear reminds me of a yellow line running down my back.

Alex Findley (10)
Newton-le-Willows Primary School, Newton-le-Willows

Fear

Fear looks like flames off a fire.
Fear smells like burnt socks.
Fear sounds like a volcano erupting in the distance.
Fear tastes like my dad's feet.
Fear feels like goosebumps running down my spine.
Fear reminds me of my brother having a bad tantrum.

Thomas Hallett (10)
Newton-le-Willows Primary School, Newton-le-Willows

Laughter

Laughter looks like a cold summer drink.
Laughter sounds like happy children having the time of their lives.
Laughter tastes like barbecue sauce.
Laughter smells like a bouquet of daffodils.
Laughter feels like a mistake turning into a crisis.
It reminds me of when I was three and I ran away from home.

Sam Tedjini (10)
Newton-le-Willows Primary School, Newton-le-Willows

Anger

Anger is red, like red-hot flames burning.
It sounds like gunshots flying through the air.
It smells like sour apples.
It looks like sparks flying through the air.
It reminds me of a bonfire on a winter's night.

Liam Haselden (10)
Newton-le-Willows Primary School, Newton-le-Willows

Anger

Anger is red like a big rocky fire.
It sounds like a big bang is going to come down.
It tastes like burning hot chilli peppers.
It smells like rotten apples.
It looks like something is going to explode.
It feels like something bad is going to happen.
It reminds me of a cat getting strangled.

Natasha Livsey
Newton-le-Willows Primary School, Newton-le-Willows

Hunger

Hunger looks like people crying,
It smells like people in starvation.
It tastes like dried up fruit,
It sounds like a distant rumbling earthquake.
It feels like a volcano in my stomach,
Hunger reminds me of children dying.

Samuel Rahaman (10)
Newton-le-Willows Primary School, Newton-le-Willows

Laughter

Laughter looks like a beautiful sun's ray,
And it reminds me of a winter's day.
Laughter smells like a beautiful flower,
And to me it would go on for hours.
Laughter feels like a fluffy cat,
And it reminds me of fun and that.

Keanu Court
Newton-le-Willows Primary School, Newton-le-Willows

Hunger

Hunger is orange like the desert.
It feels like a bubble in your tummy.
It reminds me of scrumptious food.
It looks like ripples of water.
It sounds like light thunder.
It tastes like your dreams.
It smells like barbecue.

Ashley Murphy
Newton-le-Willows Primary School, Newton-le-Willows

Guilt

Guilt is purple, like beetroot.
It looks like an egg cup.
It sounds like a loud drum.
It feels like a giant spike ball.
It smells like some mouldy cheese.
It tastes like sour sweets.
It reminds me of my worst worries.

Michael Higgins (9)
Newton-le-Willows Primary School, Newton-le-Willows

Guilt

Guilt is brown like a horse.
It tastes like brown chocolate cake.
Guilt feels like being in prison.
It reminds me of fresh air.
It sounds like someone yelling in prison.
It looks like someone being arrested.

Jack Skelton
Newton-le-Willows Primary School, Newton-le-Willows

Happiness

Happiness is white, like an angel in the sky
It feels like a soft cloud descending from Heaven.
It smells like roses growing in the fields.
It reminds me of my friends playing on the playground.
It looks like the sun smiling down at Earth.
It tastes like a raspberry freshly picked from the garden.
It sounds like the birds whistling in the summer breeze.

Leah Astbury (9)
Newton-le-Willows Primary School, Newton-le-Willows

Laughter

Laughter is white, like snowflakes falling.
Laughter tastes like jelly at Christmas.
Laughter reminds me of fun when at a party.
It feels like a soft cloud.
It smells like a bunch of daisies.
It sounds like a funny clown at the circus.
It looks like a dolphin in the sea.

Aleesha Meadows (9)
Newton-le-Willows Primary School, Newton-le-Willows

Hate

Hate is grey, like a cloud all wet and damp.
It smells like an overworked brain.
It feels like my annoying brother.
It sounds like my mum shouting at me.
It tastes like burnt toast.
It reminds me of my crying baby cousin.
It looks like an angry tiger.

Rebecca Chesworth (10)
Newton-le-Willows Primary School, Newton-le-Willows

Laughter

Laughter is yellow like happiness, all smooth and soft.
It tastes like an apple, all round and warm.
It sounds like something in your heart swaying about.
It reminds me of my birthday and we all had fun.
It feels like everyone is happy and not bad,
They are all laughing, aren't they good?
It looks like a big smile on your face.
It smelt like a clean deep breath that is starting to push out.

Estee Voong
Newton-le-Willows Primary School, Newton-le-Willows

Pride

Pride is gold like winning the FA Cup Final.
It looks like a lion strolling through the jungle.
It sounds like Thierry Henry when he scores.
It reminds me of God.
It feels like I have the power of good.
It smells like Grandma's baked bread.
It tastes like I am eating the biggest fruit cake in the world.

Daye Hardman
Newton-le-Willows Primary School, Newton-le-Willows

Anger

Anger is red, like roses in a garden.
It reminds me of love.
It tastes like hot red chillies.
It sounds like a pig snoring loudly.
It feels like a burned person.
It looks like The Terminator when he is mad.

Rachel Winstanley (9)
Newton-le-Willows Primary School, Newton-le-Willows

Autumn Days

The chilly breeze goes by, crashing into the crunchy leaves,
While the spiky conkers fall off the trees.
When the conkers are released from their spiky shells
They shine like earrings in the sun.
When the sun is shining, everyone is happy
But when the sun goes down, everyone is sad.
Now it's time to close your eyes and have a little nap.

Megan Kavanagh (7)
Newton-le-Willows Primary School, Newton-le-Willows

Silence

Silence is golden, like hot chocolate.
It reminds me of sleep.
It feels like relaxing.
It sounds like fresh air.
It smells like clear air.
It looks like bright white.

Joseph Forshaw (9)
Newton-le-Willows Primary School, Newton-le-Willows

Autumn Days

One fine autumn day
In the middle of October,
When the leaves fall from the trees,
When the birds fly high
Way up in the sky
Autumn is almost here.

Aiyshia Seebue (7)
Newton-le-Willows Primary School, Newton-le-Willows

Sadness

Sadness is dark blue, like the raging sea,
It reminds me of a broken heart,
It smells like tears,
It looks like trickles of water onto the ground,
It feels like emptiness,
It sounds like drops of water on the ocean floor,
It tastes like blood.

Bradley Swift (9)
Newton-le-Willows Primary School, Newton-le-Willows

Sadness

Sadness is a fiery red with black ash, like a city burning.
It reminds me of an atomic bomb wreaking havoc.
It feels like blood and terror trickling down my cheek.
It sounds like screams and crying.
It smells like smoke rising from destruction.
It tastes like gas and tears.
It looks like death and despair.

Joseph Botsford (9)
Newton-le-Willows Primary School, Newton-le-Willows

Darkness

Darkness is a pitch-black soul.
Darkness dwells in a fire-like hole.
Darkness is the burning leaves falling
from the dead and weary trees.
Darkness hates, lions roar as a cricket
goes on the jungle floor!

Samuel Munro Lyon (8)
Newton-le-Willows Primary School, Newton-le-Willows

Sadness

Sadness is blue
Sadness is blue, like the dark blue sea
Sadness sounds like the deep blue waves
Sadness smells like onions
Sadness feels like someone out of your heart.

Helen Robinson (9)
Newton-le-Willows Primary School, Newton-le-Willows

Happiness Is Blue

Happiness is blue, like the sky.
Happiness sounds like laughter.
Happiness smells like sweet popcorn.
Happiness feels like a big hug.

Lucy Woods (9)
Newton-le-Willows Primary School, Newton-le-Willows

Sickness

Sickness is green, like burny plop.
Sickness sounds like a wounded cat.
Sickness smells like digested pasta.
Sickness feels like a sore tum.

Rowan Lawrence
Newton-le-Willows Primary School, Newton-le-Willows

Mum And Dad

I love my mum and dad
They make me really glad
The only time they shout at me
Is when I have been bad.

Hannah Riding
Newton-le-Willows Primary School, Newton-le-Willows

Anger

Anger is black, like the dark riders.
It sounds like Hell's Angels' bikes roaring.
It smells like blood is in the air.
It feels like your head's going to burst with evil.

Jamie Boyle (9)
Newton-le-Willows Primary School, Newton-le-Willows

Joy

Joy is pink, like cherryade.
It sounds like a water slide.
It smells like chocolate being made.
Joy feels like a fairground ride.

Nicola Unsworth (8)
Newton-le-Willows Primary School, Newton-le-Willows

Happiness

Happiness is bright red, like roses.
Happiness sounds like birds tweeting.
Happiness smells like strawberry ice cream.
Happiness feels like kissing.

Abigail Byrne (8)
Newton-le-Willows Primary School, Newton-le-Willows

Anger

Anger is red, like blood
Anger sounds like people being nasty.
Anger smells like burning bodies.
Anger feels like people falling out.

Adam Hazeldine
Newton-le-Willows Primary School, Newton-le-Willows

Hate

Hate is red, like a fierce fire.
It smells like red-hot fire.
It feels like being blown up.
It sounds like a volcanic eruption.
It looks like hot air blowing.
It tastes like sour apple.

Adam Mellor (9)
Newton-le-Willows Primary School, Newton-le-Willows

Pink

Pink is the colour of paint,
Pink is a toy, furry and soft,
Pink is nice and warm,
Pink is so cute,
Pink makes me laugh,
I think pink is my favourite colour.

Louise Culling (7)
Newton-le-Willows Primary School, Newton-le-Willows

Evil

Evil is black like a thunderstorm.
Evil sounds like dark riders.
Evil smells like sewage.
Evil feels like someone's spooky hand.

Siobhan Carney
Newton-le-Willows Primary School, Newton-le-Willows

Joy

Joy is like having caring people.
Joy is like going to a cinema and having popcorn.
Joy is having fun with your friends.

Rebecca Griffiths
Newton-le-Willows Primary School, Newton-le-Willows

Happiness

Happiness is a fresh yellow, like a gleaming summer's sun.
It sounds like a spring breeze rippling through a field of roses.
It reminds me of a clear blue sky.
It looks like a sparkling sun shining over a calm river.
It smells like daffodils with pure white petals freshly grown.
It tastes like juicy, crushed strawberries.
It feels like smooth rose petals.

Jessica Judge (9)
Newton-le-Willows Primary School, Newton-le-Willows

Fear

Fear is black like a deep dark hole.
It smells like brown fresh soil.
It reminds me of a black bull with its sparkling horns.
It sounds like ghosts crying to the dead.
It tastes like rotten bananas.
It looks like a house in flames.
It feels like a stingray's skin.

Adam Bond
Newton-le-Willows Primary School, Newton-le-Willows

Hate

Hate is red, like the centre of a volcano.
It looks like two people, one being bullied.
It feels like a spiky plane after a battle.
It reminds me of fire blazing up woods.
It smells like rotten eggs.
It sounds like an engine at full blast.
It tastes like sharp lemons.

Christopher Cunliffe (9)
Newton-le-Willows Primary School, Newton-le-Willows

Happiness

Happiness is pink, like a chocolate bar.
It reminds me of a lioness playing a harp and a lovely massage.
It smells like buttercups on a farm.
It looks like frogs singing.
It feels like relaxing in a steaming sauna.
It sounds like a bee buzzing in a hive.
It tastes like red juicy strawberries.

Georgia Ivanovic (9)
Newton-le-Willows Primary School, Newton-le-Willows

Hate

Hate is like black from the dark night sky.
It feels like wind making shivers down your back.
It tastes like blood in your mouth.
It reminds me of darkness within me.
It smells like smoke in the air.
It looks like shadows coming up behind you.
It sounds like screaming from the black night.

Logan Newsome (9)
Newton-le-Willows Primary School, Newton-le-Willows

Fear

Fear is blue like the Pacific Ocean.
It looks like a big black hole.
It feels like you cannot move.
It smells like a torpedo.
It reminds me of when I was being bullied.
It tastes like gunpowder.
It sounds like a bomb.

James Parkinson
Newton-le-Willows Primary School, Newton-le-Willows

Sadness

Sadness is blue,
Like a skirt bought brand new.
It feels like a gorgeous draft of air.
It tastes of a cold snowball.
It sounds like a cool breeze.
It smells like a pure piece of leather.
It reminds me of when my cousin broke his bed.

Scott Clare
Newton-le-Willows Primary School, Newton-le-Willows

Happiness

Happiness is golden like a gold ring.
It tastes like creamy chocolate.
It feels like a rough starfish in the deep sea.
It smells like a soft, sandy sea.
It sounds like birds singing.
It looks like a squirrel jumping from tree to tree.
It reminds me of a green garden with flowers.

Cory Plant (9)
Newton-le-Willows Primary School, Newton-le-Willows

Sadness

Sadness is purple like a round plum.
It smells like the deep blue sea.
It sounds like a piano playing a sad song.
It feels like I have just fallen off a high cliff.
It looks like a heart turning to dust.
It tastes like a big currant pie.
It reminds me of when me and Nadine fell out.

Nicole Vero
Newton-le-Willows Primary School, Newton-le-Willows

Love

Love is red, like ripe raspberries.
It feels like smooth seals swimming lazily in the ocean.
It sounds like birds tweeting when dawn breaks.
It tastes like sweet strawberries growing.
It smells like fresh flowers in the garden.
It looks like a shoal of fish soaring through the sea.
It reminds me of princesses' pretty palaces surrounded
by fields full of daffodils.

Bethany Furbey (9)
Newton-le-Willows Primary School, Newton-le-Willows

Fear

Fear is black, like a shadowy storm.
It sounds like a person suffering torture.
It reminds me of pitch-black darkness at night.
It looks like a huge, looming, black spider.
It tastes like a lump of dark, damp soil.
It smells like a dead, rotting fish.
It feels like a rough, jagged, black rock.

Jamie Seddon (9)
Newton-le-Willows Primary School, Newton-le-Willows

Anger

Anger is like an abandoned ship.
It looks like a black hole.
It tastes like a horrid candy bar.
It smells like molten lava.
It sounds like a roaring dragon.
It feels like alien skin.

Asher Barry (9)
Newton-le-Willows Primary School, Newton-le-Willows

Sadness

Sadness is light blue, like the clear blue sky.
It smells like a horrible, rotten peach.
It feels like a part of you has been taken away.
It tastes like a bowl of dog food.
It looks like a cave being enclosed and someone still in it.
It sounds like a load of stones crashing into a lake.
It reminds me of a meadow that is crushed and destroyed.

Nathan Anderson (9)
Newton-le-Willows Primary School, Newton-le-Willows

Happiness

Happiness is a fresh yellow like a summer's sun.
It looks like an open spring meadow of beautiful flowers.
It reminds me of a daisy with pure white petals.
It tastes like honey fresh from the beehive.
It feels like a soft royal cushion from a princess' bed.
It smells like refreshing vanilla and lavender.
It sounds like birds singing outside your window.

Hayley Grierson
Newton-le-Willows Primary School, Newton-le-Willows

Fear

Fear is black, like dark black ash.
It tastes like burnt spare ribs.
It reminds me of when I burnt myself.
It smells like my dad's burnt black omelette.
It sounds like me when I have a mad scream.
It looks like an amazing dark door.
It feels like me having a nightmare of my dog.

Jade Waring (10)
Newton-le-Willows Primary School, Newton-le-Willows

Pink

Pink is a tulip, beautiful and bright,
Pink is an earring, shiny and bold,
Pink is a bobble, furry and soft,
Pink is a coat, dreamy and cute,
Pink is a piglet, snorty and round,
Pink is a pencil, long and hard,
Pink is a feather, smooth and ticklish,
Pink is a comic, joyful and fun,
Pink is a piece of card, firm and stiff.

Adam Philip (7)
Newton-le-Willows Primary School, Newton-le-Willows

Love

Love is pink, like a blossoming rose in summer.
It smells like the sweet scent of honeycomb.
It looks like a big bouquet of the flowers of spring.
It tastes like cooling lemonade on a hot summer's day.
It feels like a soft breeze whistling through my fingers.
It sounds like a cheerful tune played on a violin.
It reminds me of passion between a boyfriend and girlfriend.

Laura Roberts (9)
Newton-le-Willows Primary School, Newton-le-Willows

Fear

Fear looks like flames off a fire
It sounds like a volcano erupting in the distance
It smells like a really smelly egg
It tastes like gone off milk
It feels like a herd of elephants running down your spine
Fear reminds me of the first time I fell down the stairs.
(PS it hurt).

Malcolm Austin
Newton-le-Willows Primary School, Newton-le-Willows

Autumn

A ll the leaves turn brown and fall to the floor.
U nder the leaves we'll find conkers for sure.
T he days get shorter and it's colder at night.
U ntil Hallowe'en comes to give us a fright.
M any animals hibernate till spring is in sight.
N ew baby lambs then appear and the days are light.

Nathon Hollis (7)
Newton-le-Willows Primary School, Newton-le-Willows

Silence

Silence is grey, like a dull boring day.
It feels like falling from the top of a cliff.
It tastes like bad green sprouts that make your mouth dry.
It looks like a never-ending room which you cannot get out of.
It smells like cold tea which no one likes.
It reminds me of snowflakes falling silently to the ground.

Paige Melia (11)
Newton-le-Willows Primary School, Newton-le-Willows

Love!

Love looks like mushy peas
It sounds like a heart thumping rapidly
It smells like perfume
It tastes like lipstick
It feels like a fluffy bed
Love reminds me of the TV show 'Happy Days'.

Nathan Smith (10)
Newton-le-Willows Primary School, Newton-le-Willows

Laughter

Laughter smells like a bouquet of pretty summer flowers.
Laughter looks like a bunch of happy faces.
Laughter sounds like a bunch of children having a good time.
Laughter tastes like a cold summer drink.
Laughter feels like a big bubble in your stomach.
Laughter reminds me of the summertimes abroad.

Nancy Bennett
Newton-le-Willows Primary School, Newton-le-Willows

Laughter

Laughter smells like a bouquet of pretty flowers,
It sounds like a tune rising up and down,
It tastes like tonsils waggling,
It feels like jumping jelly beans,
It looks like a clown in a circus,
Laughter reminds you of playful children.

Lucy Platt (10)
Newton-le-Willows Primary School, Newton-le-Willows

Sadness

Sadness looks like a large gravestone.
Sadness smells like a burnt-out bonfire.
Sadness tastes like a spoonful of salt.
Sadness sounds like a child crying in the distance.
Sadness feels like a brick in your heart's desire.
Sadness reminds me of a sad part in life.

Kealan R-Smith (10)
Newton-le-Willows Primary School, Newton-le-Willows

Love

Love looks like a giant heart ringing,
Love smells like a lovely red rose,
It tastes like a cup of tea and a chocolate biscuit,
It sounds like a heart thumping rapidly,
Love feels like warmth and security,
Love reminds me of life.

Scott Reilly (10)
Newton-le-Willows Primary School, Newton-le-Willows

Happiness

Happiness is yellow, like the shining sparkly sun.
It feels like joy in the world.
It tastes like hot chocolate fudge cake.
It smells like freshly cut grass in the garden.
It reminds me of my baby nephew.

Adam Roberts (10)
Newton-le-Willows Primary School, Newton-le-Willows

Love

Love looks like a big red heart,
Love smells like nice perfume,
Love sounds like a heart thumping rapidly,
Love tastes like chocolate melting in your mouth,
Love feels like a pink fluffy pillow,
Love reminds me of a field of red roses.

Lauren Kilshaw (11)
Newton-le-Willows Primary School, Newton-le-Willows

Love!

Love looks like a huge rose swaying gently in the breeze.
It smells like sherbet on hot strawberries.
It sounds like a heart thumping rapidly.
It tastes like sweet candy canes hanging on the tree.
Love feels like a soft, pink, fluffy slipper.
Love reminds you of two little lovebirds whistling way up high.

Katie Hovvels (11)
Newton-le-Willows Primary School, Newton-le-Willows

Love!

Love is blue like a big, fluffy cloud dancing in the sky.
It feels like birds fluttering inside.
It tastes like candyfloss at a playground fair.
It smells like honey because honey's so sweet.
It reminds me of my mum giving me a kiss goodnight.

Charlotte Stein (11)
Newton-le-Willows Primary School, Newton-le-Willows

Fun

Fun is pink, like pretty high heels in a shop!
It feels like fluffy pink pillows!
It looks like the Trafford Centre!
It smells like perfume on my mum when she goes out!
It tastes like chocolate!
It reminds me of shopping.

Lucy Crean (10)
Newton-le-Willows Primary School, Newton-le-Willows

Happiness

Happiness is like tomato soup in a bubbling pan.
It feels like walking on newborn sand.
It tastes like freshly grown strawberries which have just
Fallen off a plant.
It looks like horses playing in the sea.
It smells like a lovely perfume crushed from roses and tulips.
It reminds me of my first day of Y5 in this school.

Chelsey Oakes
Newton-le-Willows Primary School, Newton-le-Willows

Love

Love is red like the blazing sun,
It feels like your heart is in your mouth,
It tastes like strawberries and cream,
It looks like bubbles floating in the air,
It smells like a lovely perfume,
It reminds me of all my happy memories.

Bethany Vizard
Newton-le-Willows Primary School, Newton-le-Willows

Fear

Fear is black, like a creepy spider,
It feels like creepy-crawlies in my stomach,
It tastes like fire inside my mouth pounding like a drum,
It looks like cars in a fire pit,
It smells like an evil devil in my chest,
It reminds me of my worst nightmare.

Kayleigh Aspinwall (11)
Newton-le-Willows Primary School, Newton-le-Willows

Darkness!

Darkness is black like a bat cave.
It feels like you're outside in the cold,
It tastes like burnt toast,
It looks like an old haunted house,
It smells like rotten eggs.
It reminds me of a scary film on a rainy night.

Danielle Williams
Newton-le-Willows Primary School, Newton-le-Willows

Fear

Fear is black like a dark stormy night.
It feels like you're on your own and nobody likes you.
It tastes like fire exploding inside you.
It looks like cars exploding around you.
It smells like burning wood around you.
It reminds you of all your bad memories.

Tiffany Eccles
Newton-le-Willows Primary School, Newton-le-Willows

Sadness

Sadness looks like the ten o'clock news,
It sounds like small children weeping,
It smells like a burnt cake in the oven,
It tastes like gone off milk,
It feels like being bored,
Sadness reminds me of people being killed.

Sarah Gordon-Simpson
Newton-le-Willows Primary School, Newton-le-Willows

Sadness

Sadness looks like the sun going down
at the end of a joyful day.

Sadness smells like something burning
in the oven.

Sadness sounds like small children weeping.

Sadness tastes like a burnt pie.

Sadness feels like a thunderstorm making the day
dull and grey.

It reminds me of the colour blue.

Louise Clare (10)
Newton-le-Willows Primary School, Newton-le-Willows

Playtime

Playtime comes each and every day,
When the bell goes we can't wait to play.
We like to play skipping, tig and running away.
My best mate was skipping when she tripped up and fell,
And when she got up Miss rang the bell.
So playtime started with the ring of a bell,
Today it finished when my best mate fell.

Megan Canning (9)
St Columba's Catholic Primary School, Huyton

The Ocean

The ocean is beautiful and calm but can be dangerous.
The ocean is swaying, soothing and relaxing
Like a man blowing on the water.

The ocean is like a flat bed, and it makes me relaxed.
The ocean is beautiful and calm but can be dangerous.

The ocean was here before land.

Lea Courtney, Liam Metcalfe (8) Michael Scales (10)
St Columba's Catholic Primary School, Huyton

Food

Bacon, tomatoes, pickles and peas,
I'll have those for my breakfast please.

Spaghetti, noodles, cheese on toast,
Which one do I like the most?

And what should I have in-between?
Crisps, chocolate or a tangerine?

What about for my tea?
Burger, chips or a fish from the sea?
Washed down with lemonade,
I'll drink that or Minute Maid.

For dessert I might choose to eat . . .
A banana split or another treat.

That food was really yummy,
But I've got food in my tummy.

I'm starting to feel really sick pass me a
Bucket and make it *quick!*

Rebecca Darracott (10)
St Columba's Catholic Primary School, Huyton

The Rain

The rain never stops in winter
The rain is heavy, dull and miserable
The rain is like a teardrop of a little child
It swoops down really wild
The rain is sometimes fun
When you skip, jump and run
The rain is like a big *splash*
The falling rain.

Nicola Sullivan & Lauren Sothern (10)
St Columba's Catholic Primary School, Huyton

The Sparkling Jewellery

The sparkling jewellery,
A woman's best friend,
Sparkling, shining and glimmery,
Like a sparkle in a woman's eye,
Like a river reflecting,
It makes me feel like a princess,
Like a million pounds,
The sparkling jewellery,
Reminds us of what a special present it could be.

Kimberley Dooley, Natalie Dooley & Lauren Cassells (10)
St Columba's Catholic Primary School, Huyton

The Pirates

The pirates on the gloomy ship.
Many centuries ago.
Huge, hunted, blood.
Travelling to unknown.
Like the skeleton in the dark.
It makes me feel afraid and horrified.
Like a ship that no one can see or hear
The great disturbing ship
Reminds us how long our life is.

Nicola Jones & Jessica Gardner (10)
St Columba's Catholic Primary School, Huyton

The Foggy Day

One foggy day in Sefton Park
I heard a dog begin to bark
He barked so loud he barked so long
I asked the owner what was wrong
'He's scared of fog,' his owner said
'I think he'd rather be in bed.'
I laughed out loud at this remark
And made my way home from the park
When I got home at half-past eight
My mum was waiting at the gate
'Where have you been in all this fog?'
'Oh just laughing at a foggy dog.'

Laura Fitzsimmons (9)
St Columba's Catholic Primary School, Huyton

The Wind

The fierce wind
Can destroy buildings
Freezing, powerful, evil
Like a man whistling in your ear
Shouting at the top of his voice
It makes me shiver
I feel like a leaf getting blown away
The fierce wind
Makes me feel
Powerless.

Joe Bennett & Kyle Hughes (10)
St Columba's Catholic Primary School, Huyton

Anger

I feel so angry I feel so sad
Everybody thinks I'm bad.

Why do they judge and tease me so?
I just can't wait for this phase to go.

Why does anger build up in me?
Why doesn't anger come out in anyone I can see?

Anger is like a raging ball of fire
It is definitely not my desire.

Amanda Coughlan (10)
St Columba's Catholic Primary School, Huyton

Fireworks

Bright sparks fly from the sky,
Rockets bang, crowd 'ooohs' and 'aaahs'.
'This is great,' they cry
'It's like falling stars, flying through the sky.'
The thrill of the rides
And all the yummy food.
This must be firework night.

*'Remember, remember the fifth of November
Gunpowder, treason and plot.
I see no reason why gunpowder treason
Should ever be forgot'.*
This must be firework night.

Firework night
One of my favourite nights.
This must be firework night.

Charlotte Atherton (10)
Sunnymede School, Southport

The Hallowe'en Witch

The Hallowe'en witch flies through the town,
On her broomstick in her dressing gown,
Round the buildings up and down,
Knocking on the windows, knocking on the doors,
Of all the massive quick save stores,
Stealing all the sweets, stealing all the treats,
And eats them all up with just one gobble,
She soon started to feel wheezy and wobble,
But that was a long time ago,
When all things were scary and so,
The Hallowe'en witch does this no more,
Because she works in the old quick save store,
She'll still come back on Hallowe'en
Even though she's not quite so keen.

Faye Liley (9)
Sunnymede School, Southport

Football

Football, oh football
How I love thee.
Football oh football
My name is Lee
Football oh football
I am filled with glee.
Football oh football
Now I leave you happily
Football, oh football
But who doesn't?
I know -
The referee.

George Alexander (9)
Sunnymede School, Southport

Shopping Trolley

My shopping trolley
I put in the keys
And ram it into the back of someone's knees

Go over a ramp and land somewhere damp
And soak them until they fall on the ground
And mother them until they give you a pound.

You really won't believe your eyes
My trolley's been specialised
It's got a hummer chassis
It has a sport seat and
All round the store watch out for your feet.

It's got chrome rims with diamond screws
It is now going to be on the news.

Alasdair Mitchell (9)
Sunnymede School, Southport

Dopey Dan

Dopey Dan
Is a dopey man

Every morning he
Gets hit by a frying pan

He runs like a lamb
And loves his gran.

He goes to the pub
And gets a good rub.

Then he will get in the tub
And have a good scrub
He's on the football team as a sub.

Dopey Dan has a duck
And is a very good cook
That's why he's stuck in a storybook.

Grace Robertson (9)
Sunnymede School, Southport

Ghosts

Ghosts are here
Ghosts are there
But try not
To say
Ghosts aren't
Anywhere
They'll sneak up
At night
And hit you
Like a lightning strike
If you have
Second eyesight
You'll get a bit
Of a fright
Try to hit them
You'll get nowhere
Ghosts are here
Ghosts are there
But try not
To say
Ghosts
Aren't
Anywhere.

Ellie Mawdsley (9)
Sunnymede School, Southport

Shopping Trolley

If you say 'Please' I will ram into the back of your knees
Put in the keys and you'll never say, 'Eat Chinese.'
Go up a ramp and you'll land somewhere damp
You really won't believe your eyes because my
Trolley's been magnetized
It's got a Zonda chassis and a velvet seat
Shopping with my trolley is quite a feat.

Giles Mawdsley (10)
Sunnymede School, Southport

Whatever I Want

W hatever I say, I never get what I want.
H appy or sad, I never get what I want.
A lways or never, I just don't get what I want.
T o or fro, I never get what I want.
E ven or odd, I never get what I want.
V enturing or adventurous, I never get what I want.
E veryone or no one, I never get what I want.
R eading or racing, I never get what I want.

I never get what I want.

W ellies or trainers, I never get what I want.
A ce or bad, I never get what I want.
N ever, ever, ever.
T en or eleven, I never get what I want.

I never get what I want.

N ormal or mad, I never get what I want.
E verything or nothing, I never get what I want.
V icar or maid, I never get what I want.
E xample or question, I never get what I want.
R olling or tumbling, I never get what I want.

G enie or builders, I never get what I want.
E xtensions or short, I just never get what I want.
T oday I got what I wanted, but I don't want it anymore.

Bethany Ferns (10)
Sunnymede School, Southport

Angry

Angry is red like my parents get when I get in trouble.
Angry sounds loud like when people shout at me.
Angry really hurts my feelings because I don't like
people shouting at me.
Anger smells like fear to me.
But I guess we will have to see.

Michael Speed (10)
Sunnymede School, Southport

My Dog

My dog never bites
When someone flicks him on the nose
My dog never bites
When someone pushes him over
My dog never bites
When someone takes away his food
My dog never bites
But when a robber comes through the door
Then he'll have a go.

My dog loves a tickle
When someone comes through the door
My dog loves a tickle
When someone is at the table
My dog loves a tickle
When some is watching TV
My dog loves a tickle
But when you have a biscuit then he'll get up and eat it.

My dog loves a sleep
In the day and in the night
My dog loves a sleep
When you want to play football with him
My dog loves a sleep
But when you want to play with his favourite toy
Up he jumps to play with me.

Lewis Houlgrave (10)
Sunnymede School, Southport

Dippee Duck

Dippee duck is a crook
Dippee duck loves his book
Dippee duck eats his ducks
Dippee duck gets away by luck
Dippee duck hates to cook
Dippee duck loves to look.

Aidan Harrison (9)
Sunnymede School, Southport

Hope

Hope is caused by Sadness inside
Building up like a rising tide.

Then when one opens it up like a book
It no longer wants to be closed back up.

And when it flourishes Hope is made
So Sadness' greed is greatly delayed.

Thomas Griffin-Lea (10)
Sunnymede School, Southport

Bored

Bored is black like an ancient tomb.
Bored is quiet like a room with nothing in it.
Bored is horrible like eating a lemon.
Bored is thick like moving your fingers through a brush.
Bored is smelly like a stench coming from a horse.

Jack Morris-Holland (10)
Sunnymede School, Southport

Boredom

Bored is like a belch coming from a big mouth.
Bored is like eating chocolate cake with sauce.
Bored is like smelling peanut butter.
Bored is like touching a blunt sword.
Bored is the colour of black darkness.

Adam Galley (10)
Sunnymede School, Southport

Embarrassed

Embarrassed is pink, like when you're spotted wearing it,
And you're a boy, so you get laughed at more than a bit.

Embarrassed is quiet, when you don't know what to do,
Like when you called an elephant, a lion at the zoo.

Embarrassed is stale, like the bread Mum made,
Then she gave it to the headmaster and I got a bad grade.

Embarrassed is rough like the luck I get,
But when you're embarrassed what more could you expect?

Joe Mansour (10)
Sunnymede School, Southport

Bored

Bored is black like when you are asleep.
Bored is quiet like when everyone you know is fast asleep.
Bored is dry as if you are feeding on a sandy beach.
Bored is just like nothing.
Bored is just like the dentist's waiting room.

Adam Finnigan (10)
Sunnymede School, Southport

Bored

Bored is black like someone sleeping.
Bored is someone talking for ages.
Bored is a rubbery taste.
Bored is when you can't touch anything.

Edward Rigby (10)
Sunnymede School, Southport

The Zoo

Wild animals roaring and barking
Tigers running, jumping the parrots are squawking.
Koalas and monkeys hanging in a nearby tree.
Beluga whales and elephants are all bigger than me.
Mantises and killer bees are in the bug section.
Two white rhinos have escaped and now the zoo is trying to catch them.
Chimpanzees are picking fleas off other monkey's backs.
It's feeding time for the great white sharks.
The stingrays are stinging the little silver fishes.
The stingrays are serving them up on stone dishes.
The gorillas are having a wrestling match.
Then the lion rips a bit of hair out of his mane,
which leaves him with a humungous patch.
So that's where I leave the zoo.
Zoo, zoo, zoo wonderful zoo.

Jack Cope (9)
Sunnymede School, Southport

The Cinema

You arrive at the cinema shouting and screaming,
Purses and wallets at the ready for getting popcorn.
People teaming up to buy the tickets for the horror movie,
All blood and guts when White Nancy is at the scene.
I remember the first time I saw it, I jumped right out of my skin!
My hand was shaking when I held the Coke,
Screaming, shouting, 'Help, oh help!'
That night, I got nightmares about the cinema,
No more horror movies for me.
I'll stick to Disney, thanks,
That was a good day at the cinema for White Nancy and me!

Georgina Williams (10)
Sunnymede School, Southport

In And Out

In and out, all about
Round and round, up and down.

They're watching a lark, in the park.
What a beautiful day,
Oh yay.

In this time no need to commit a crime.

Watch for the sunshine,
Slap on your cream, and don't be mean.

Don't spoil it now on the wonderful day
Let's just play.

Cassie Kelly-Donoghue (9)
Sunnymede School, Southport

The Magic Box
(Based on 'Magic Box' by Kit Wright)

I will put in the box . . .
A flying merry-go-round
A turquoise flying sausage.
A naked moose.

I will put in the box . . .
A shark head on a lion
A swinging sandwich
Miss McEneany in a tuxedo and Mr Parry in a cardigan.

My box is made from . . .
Water from River Thames
Bones from the dead.

In my box I will . . .
Drown ugly fish
Go crazy.

Jonathan Wild (7)
Waterloo Primary School, Liverpool

What Would You Choose?

When I am happy
I think of my friends.
When I see my friends I feel excited
I get the taste of sugar dummies
I hear people laughing and jumping
I can smell the salty sea
What would you choose?

Megan Ward (8)
Waterloo Primary School, Liverpool

The Day I Got In Trouble

When I do something bad my dad shouts at me
I feel scared when my dad shouts
He goes very dark red
He looks fierce like a bull
I hate that day when my dad shouts at me!

Holly McGhee (8)
Waterloo Primary School, Liverpool

The Anger

The sound is like shouting
It reminds me of the time when I lost my temper
It smells horrible like cowpat
I feel sad and fierce when I use it
The taste is like a monster's breath.
It looks annoying and the colours are black and blue.

Georgia Smith (9)
Waterloo Primary School, Liverpool

What Is Funny?

Jokes are funny and children burst out with laughter
It tastes like the creamiest ice cream and toffee chocolate
It smells like fresh cornflakes in the morning
When you're ready for a fresh start.

The children's mouths of laughter
Are as big as a giraffes.
The colour of laughter is yellow as the yellow, fire-breathing sun

It makes me feel like I am asleep in the dark night sky
It reminds me of a car breaking down.

Aimee Hughes (8)
Waterloo Primary School, Liverpool

The Happy Lad Of Waterloo

The happy lad of Waterloo,
Sang with birds and hamsters too
With every blue sky
He made a sweet pie.
For every animal of Waterloo.

Ben Cook (8)
Waterloo Primary School, Liverpool

Calmness

When it's silent I hear breathing and *taste* the air
When it's silent I smell my dad's coffee floating in the air
I see the blue sky then I start to cry and relax my head too.

Rebecca Swinnerton (8)
Waterloo Primary School, Liverpool

The Weather

A sun is like a shining pancake high up in the sky.
A cloud is like a fluffy pillow floating in the sky.
The puddles from the rain are like little rivers on the ground,
The rain is like teardrops falling from the sky.
The wind is like a big giant fan blowing you,
A rainbow is like a colourful bridge high up in the sky.

Melissa Clarke (8)
Waterloo Primary School, Liverpool

Calm

The sea is calm
You are calm
Look at the sea
See the sea
Whoosh, whoosh, swish
Blue, wavy seas.

Valerie Anirah (8)
Waterloo Primary School, Liverpool

Happy

Happiness is bright yellow
It sounds like laughter
Happiness tastes like the wildest fruits
It smells like daisies blowing in the breeze.
Happiness looks like smiling faces
It feels joyful, merry and blissful
Happiness reminds me of the sun shining.

Katy Maybury (11)
Waterloo Primary School, Liverpool

Happiness

Happiness is yellow
It sounds like children laughing
Happiness tastes like a packet of sweets from the shop
It smells like food
Happiness looks like smiles all around
It feels like kicking a football
Happiness reminds me of the time when I got my dog.

Alex Kershaw (10)
Waterloo Primary School, Liverpool

Love

Love is red
It sounds like the sea coming up the beach
Love tastes like the juiciest watermelon ever
Smells like soft mint
Looks like the moon in the night sky.
Feels like squidgy Play-Doh
Reminds me of roast dinner.

Sam Cook (10)
Waterloo Primary School, Liverpool

Animals

A monkey is like a vine
A zebra is like a stripy sock
A snake is like a worm
A starfish is like a star
A leopard is like a spotty hairband.

Kelsey Cunnah (8)
Waterloo Primary School, Liverpool

Anger

Anger's colour is fresh blood dripping from the bathroom wall
Anger sounds like a screaming woman
Anger tastes like smoke burning down my throat
Anger smells like a dog's breath
Anger looks like fire-breathing dragons
Anger feels like daggers cutting your heart out
Anger reminds me of RIP signs.

Molly O'Callaghan (10)
Waterloo Primary School, Liverpool

Love

Love is red and pink
It sounds like wedding bells
Love tastes like chocolate melting in my mouth
It smells like roses
It looks like caramel
It feels like holding a newborn baby
Love reminds me of sitting by Katy Maybury by the lovely, warm fire.

Karim Benallal (10)
Waterloo Primary School, Liverpool

Love

Love is red
It sounds like a piano playing
Love tastes like chocolate fizzing
It smells like pink roses being watered
Love looks like sparkling stars
It feels like a baby's bottom
Love reminds me of my bed.

Natalie Brazendale (10)
Waterloo Primary School, Liverpool

Happiness

Happiness is red
It sounds like children laughing
Happiness tastes like chocolate
It smells like bluebells in the meadow
Happiness looks like children running around
It feels like joy in my heart
Happiness reminds me of the best day of my life.

Rachel Bellamy (10)
Waterloo Primary School, Liverpool

Jealousy

Jealousy is green
It sounds like pure disgrace
Jealousy tastes bitter and spicy all around
It smells like seaweed washed up on the shore.
Jealousy looks like rubbish piled high up into the sky
It feels like you live in sadness and not a smile around
Jealousy reminds me of loneliness and not a soul around.

Joanne Tasker (10)
Waterloo Primary School, Liverpool

Love

Love is red
It sounds like wedding bells,
Love tastes like chocolate in my mouth.
Love smells like a poppy in a greenhouse.
Love looks like people dancing happily.
Love feels like soft rose petals
Love reminds me of a heart.

Luke Macaulay (10)
Waterloo Primary School, Liverpool

Clowning Around

Funniness is all around me
Because all the clowning around
Yum-yum, mouth-watering candyfloss and popcorn.
All I can smell is Mr G's smelly socks
How can it be? Oh it's Goofy
All I can see is multicoloured dots
I feel swishy all inside but I don't know why.

Hannah Stevens (8)
Waterloo Primary School, Liverpool

Love

Love is a red rose
It sounds like a wedding song
Love tastes like chocolate hearts
It smells like bluebells in fields
Love looks like the stars
It feels like a hug off my mum
Love reminds me of a baby.

Andy Gilbert (11)
Waterloo Primary School, Liverpool

Happy

Happiness is bright orange
It sounds like laughter
Happiness tastes like Sunny-D
It smells like a basket of roses
Happiness looks like children having fun
It feels like you're playing games.
Happiness reminds me of my family.

Emma Brie (10)
Waterloo Primary School, Liverpool

My Teacher

Mr Parry is gold
Mr Parry is a summer morning
Mr Parry is a windy storm
Mr Parry is a gym
Mr Parry is a tuxedo
Mr Parry is a warm, soapy bath
Mr Parry is a boss singer for the X-Factor
Mr Parry is spicy lemon custard.

Ryan Maybury (7)
Waterloo Primary School, Liverpool

My Teacher

Miss McEneany is yellow
She is a summer afternoon
She is the boiling sun
She is at the beach
She is high heels
She is a tidy bed
She is EastEnders
She is a chicken burger.

Leah Bryant (7)
Waterloo Primary School, Liverpool

My Teacher

Mr Parry is bright, white
He is a winter's evening
Watching TV in his house
He is soft snowy day
He is a stripy colour jumper
He is Tom and Jerry
He is saucy spaghetti.

Ellen Ashcroft (7)
Waterloo Primary School, Liverpool

The Magic Box
(Based on 'Magic Box' by Kit Wright)

I will put in the box . . .
A footballer playing rugby
A rugby player playing footie
A lion dancing.

I will put in the box . . .
A ballerina being lazy
A baby doing the washing
A man sleeping in a cot.

My box is made out of . . .
A big baby's head
The hinges were made out of chains.

In my box I will . . .
Go to Devon to get a takeaway
And eat it on the beach.

Lee Clarke (7)
Waterloo Primary School, Liverpool

My Teacher

Mr Parry is red
He is a summer morning
He is a heavy hailstone
He is a hot beach
He is a warm woolly jumper
He is a tidy bed
He is match of the day
He is chicken fried rice.

Katie McCollah (7)
Waterloo Primary School, Liverpool

The Magic Box
(Based on 'Magic Box' by Kit Wright)

I will put in the box . . .

Eyes with cobwebs around
A witch with a thorn in her nose,
Miss McEneany with a moustache.

I will put in the box . . .

A dog's body and a buffalo's head,
A shark in Egypt
A pig on a trampoline.

My box is made from . . .
Magnets covered in frog's eyes,
The hinges are vampire's teeth.

In my box I will . . .
Swim with sharks in Tenerife,
Meet Elvis.

Stephanie Joy (7)
Waterloo Primary School, Liverpool

My Teacher

Miss Holmes is pink
Miss Holmes is a bright, summer-yellow sun
She lives in a lovely, fantastic, flowery house
She is a nice sparkling dress
She is a soft, snowy-white settee
She is Coronation Street.
She is vanilla ice cream topped with cherry sauce and a Flake.

Rosie Biggar (7)
Waterloo Primary School, Liverpool

The Magic Box
(Based on 'Magic Box' by Kit Wright)

I will put in the box . . .

A big sticky lollipop,
A barking mummy and a dead dog.
A fat monkey and a swinging pig.

I will put in the box . . .

Mr Parry in a silky ballgown
Mrs McEneany in a bow tie
A Chinese dragon's nostril.

My box is made from . . .
A sheepskin
The lock is made from music.

In my box I will . . .
Lick my lollipop
Look at the dead dog.

Lauren Burdell (7)
Waterloo Primary School, Liverpool

Happiness

Happiness sounds like birds tweeting
Happiness tastes like strawberry ice cream
Happiness smells like red roses.
Happiness feels like a fluffy cat
Happiness reminds me of the sun.

Happiness is playing in a swimming pool
Happiness is running on a field
Happiness is a smiling, skiing, silly snake.
Happiness makes me feel like a buzzing bee.

Daniel Ritson (7)
Waterloo Primary School, Liverpool

The Magic Box
(Based on 'Magic Box' by Kit Wright)

I will put in the box . . .

A flying blue pig
A bouncing fat dog
A skinny hairy bear.

I will put in the box . . .

A greedy green frog
A grey, big, blue lion
A dead dog and cat.

My box is made out of . . .

Gold from a special king
Wood from a ruined forest tree.

In my box I will . . .

Create a world champion boxer
I will meet Michael Jackson.

Kieran Jones (8)
Waterloo Primary School, Liverpool

My Teacher

Miss Holmes is lovely beautiful lilac,
She is boiling hot summer,
She is sunny and hot.
She lives in a lovely house with flowers around it.
She is a fantastic long skirt,
She is an unmade bed.
She is the X-Factor
She is spaghetti Bolognese.

Bronwyn Richardson (7)
Waterloo Primary School, Liverpool

The Magic Box
(Based on 'Magic Box' by Kit Wright)

I will put in the box . . .
A yellow tortoise with spots,
A flying cat with purple spots,
A tiny hamster with green hair.

I will put in the box . . .
Hot dog covered in gravy
A T-shirt made from wood.

My box is made from . . .
Dogs' skin
The hinges are made from dinosaur claws.

In my box I will . . .
Travel to Jamaica on a donkey,
Meet Shaggy from Scooby-Doo.

Alexandra Holmes (7)
Waterloo Primary School, Liverpool

My Teacher

Mr Parry is red,
He is an autumn afternoon,
He is a heavy thunderstorm,
He is a red Liverpool kit,
He is a soapy sink,
He is a Ready Steady Cook
He is a spicy chicken soup.

Miss Holmes is bright green
She is a winter afternoon playing in the snow
She is shiny shoes
She is a messy couch
She is EastEnders
She is spicy chicken.

Robbie Gourlay (8)
Waterloo Primary School, Liverpool

The Magic Box
(Based on 'Magic Box' by Kit Wright)

I will put in the box . . .
A gorgeous smile from my sister
A flying sausage, a giant, huge dinosaur.

I will put in the box . . .
Miss McEneany with a tie on,
Mr Parry with high heels!
Miss Holmes giving out chance tickets.

My box is made from . . .
Metal from a cave in Ireland,
It is covered in kangaroo skin.

In my box I will . . .
Travel to Scotland,
Ride a brown horse that can jump 5 miles.

Olivia Morris (7)
Waterloo Primary School, Liverpool

The Magic Box
(Based on 'Magic Box' by Kit Wright)

I will put in the box . . .
Miss Holmes in boots and tie
A fat brown dog
Yellow happy hippo.

I will put in my box . . .
A little fat chicken
A big, fat, bouncing bear
A spotty chicken nugget.

My box is made from . . .
Egyptian sand.
The hinges are a witch's hand.

In my box I will . . .
Go to the shop with £1,000.

Josh Martin (7)
Waterloo Primary School, Liverpool

Happiness

Happiness is orange like juice.
Happiness sounds like a train going along the track.
Happiness tastes like my favourite toffee yoghurt.
Happiness smells like just cooked toast.
Happiness looks like my lovely mummy.
Happiness feels like going to the shops with Mum.

Michael Wainwright (9)
Waterloo Primary School, Liverpool

Fear

Fear is black like a dark shadow.
Fear sounds like chattering teeth.
Fear tastes like vampire blood.
Fear smells like ugly witch.
Fear looks like slimy slug.
Fear feels like sticky slobber.

Andrew Jones (10)
Waterloo Primary School, Liverpool

Anger

Anger is blue like a bus
Anger sounds like a siren.
Angers tastes like sour sweets
Angers smells like bad tomatoes
Anger looks like a lion.
Anger feels like a sword.

Matthew Liggett (7)
Waterloo Primary School, Liverpool

Fear

Fear is black, like the night
Fear sounds like a ghost's creepy voice
Fear tastes like blood
Fear smells like stinky feet
Fear looks like three bloody eyes.
Fear feels like a wriggly spider.

Abbie Weedall (9)
Waterloo Primary School, Liverpool

Anger

Anger is red, like a fire engine
Anger sounds like a noisy train.
Anger tastes like a horrible roast dinner
Anger smells like bad fish.
Anger looks like a green frog
Anger feels like a punch in the tummy.

Luke Williams (8)
Waterloo Primary School, Liverpool

Fear

Fear is red like fire
Fear sounds like vampires shouting
Fear tastes like ghost's slime
Fear smells like green gas
Fear looks like a devil monster
Fear feels like spiky spiders.

Mark Lythgoe (9)
Waterloo Primary School, Liverpool

Happiness

Happiness is blue like a bright sky
Happiness sounds like the music from my favourite video.
Happiness tastes like sausage rolls from Sayers.
Happiness smells like buttered toast.
Happiness looks like my big sister
Happiness feels like stroking my three dogs.

Scott Pursall (7)
Waterloo Primary School, Liverpool

Fear

Fear is black like a witch
Fear sounds like scary music
Fear tastes like eyeballs
Fear smells like horrible peas
Fear looks like a scary tree
Fear feels like a spider's web.

Abbie Larkin (8)
Waterloo Primary School, Liverpool

The Weather

The sun is like a giant bowling ball on fire
Rain is like giant teardrops
The clouds are like mash
Wind is like giant's breath
Snow is like icy bouncy balls
Rainbows are like colourful bridges.

Jack McCourt (8)
Waterloo Primary School, Liverpool

Love

Love sounds like dolphins leaping out of the water.
Love tastes like chocolate pudding with ice cream.
Love smells like a bunch of bright red roses.
Love feels like a nice, soft, comfy bed.
Love reminds me of angels flying in Heaven.
Love is full of hearts.
Love is like puppies crawling all over you.
Love is like lovely, laughing, leaping leopards.
Love makes me feel like birds flying in the breeze.

Emma Foy (8)
Waterloo Primary School, Liverpool

Animals

Dogs are like pillows
Zebras are like grass
Penguins are like fish
Lions are like monsters
Spiders are like hairballs
Kangaroos are like jumping jacks.

Toni Dolan (8)
Waterloo Primary School, Liverpool

Animals

A zebra is like a stripy sock
A camel's hump is like a hill
A spider is like a hairy hedgehog
A stick insect is like a piece of grass
A dog is like a furry coat
A snake is like a slimy snail.

Jake Strickland (9)
Waterloo Primary School, Liverpool

Happiness

Happiness makes me feel like a sunflower
Happiness feels like a soft cloud
Happiness is like a beautiful piano making sounds
Happiness is when you see the sun
Happiness is when you look at the blue sky
Happiness tastes like a cake in my mouth
Happiness is smelling some chocolate
Happiness reminds me of beautiful things.

Shannon Traynier
Waterloo Primary School, Liverpool

The Weather

Rain is like peardrops falling from the sky,
A cloud is like a floating sheep high up in the sky.
Snow is like ice cubes that make you very cold,
A rainbow is like a bridge with a pot of gold.
Fog is like fluff that clouds the sky,
The wind is like a giant sneeze from someone high above.

Jenny Glen (8)
Waterloo Primary School, Liverpool

Weather

The sun is like a pancake
The clouds are like furry coats,
The rain is like little pears
The clouds are like a comfortable bed
The moon is like a football
The wind is like a whisper in the air.

Jamie Woodward (9)
Waterloo Primary School, Liverpool

Happiness

If happiness is me
Then happiness can be as sweet as a hot summer's day
If happiness was greater than nature I don't know what I would do
If happiness was greater then nature I would be happier than you
A breeze of happiness on a winter's day
A breeze of happiness goes all the way
If only my happiness could be, I think it is, greater than nature.

Rachel Buckley (8)
Waterloo Primary School, Liverpool

Anger

When I am angry
I kick and scream and cry.
I don't mean to
I just can't help it
I take it out like this
I kick and scream and cry
It's not fair
I just want to say
'Stop it or I'll kick and scream and cry.'

Rachel Gilbert
Waterloo Primary School, Liverpool

I'm Angry

When I'm angry I'm upset
I cry like I have a tantrum and jump on my bed
But I pretend I'm so upset -
I'm as angry as a rhino,
I'm like a lightning bolt searching for happiness
I go as red as the sun.
I kick, cry and scream like I'm not happy.

Abby Scott (8)
Waterloo Primary School, Liverpool

Birthday

It's my birthday soon and I can't wait,
I've invited all my mates.
When it's my party I'll be so kind.
Jelly or ice cream I can't make up my mind.
Everyone will be there at my house including
The cat, the dog and the mouse.
At my party nothing will go wrong
Because all my tables are nice and strong,
On my birthday no one will shed a tear.

Caitlin Lythgoe (8)
Waterloo Primary School, Liverpool

What Is Sad?

Sad is grey
It sounds like slow constant crying
Sad tastes like salty tears trickling down someone's face
It smells like traffic fumes by a busy road
Sad looks like a puddle with raindrops falling into it.
It feels like cold bed quilts in an empty room
Sad reminds me of a single church bell sobbing on its own.

Paul Fuller (10)
Waterloo Primary School, Liverpool

Weather

The rainbow is like a colourful world
The rain is like ice cream dripping
The rain feels like someone crying
The clouds feel like fluffy beds.

Hannah Spencer (8)
Waterloo Primary School, Liverpool

Love

Love is red
It sounds like Katy Maybury kissing me
Love tastes like chocolate
It smells like perfume of your girlfriend
Love looks like shooting stars at night
It feels like scoring a hat-trick in football
Love reminds me of 'Bo Selecta!'

Joel Chapman (11)
Waterloo Primary School, Liverpool

Friendship

'Friend'
Friendship, friendship I'm nothing without friendship
Without you I'm dust
Please help me
I am the person to trust
And without you I'm teased
So help me past the strong breeze.

Lewis Kirby (8)
Waterloo Primary School, Liverpool

Food

A pizza is like a frisbee because it's round and flat
An apple is like a tennis ball
A banana is like a wonky bridge
Spaghetti is like string in big knots
Curry is like spices of meat.

John Hearfield (8)
Waterloo Primary School, Liverpool

What Is Pink?
(Based on 'What Is Pink?' by Christina Rossetti)

What is pink? Pigs are pink,
Rolling around and having a drink,
What is red? A fire is red,
Burning brightly until I go to bed.
What is blue? The sea is blue,
Ready for ships to sail through.
What is yellow? The sun is yellow,
Big and warm and mellow
What is white? Sugar is white,
Nice for your cup of tea at night.
What is green? Trees are green.
Growing big and easily seen.
What is violet? The stars are violet
Very bright in the twilight sky.
What is orange? A bean is orange
Just a baked bean.

Amy Evans (10)
Wellesbourne School, Norris Green

What Is Pink?
(Based on 'What Is Pink?' by Christina Rossetti)

What is pink? My toe is pink
When it is in the sink.
What is red? My blood is red
When I've cut my head.
What is blue? The sky is blue
Just like my tissue,
What is white? My bread is white,
When I go to have a bite.
What is yellow? A bananas yellow
Which tastes beautifully mellow
What is violet? A plant is violet
When it twinkles in the twilight
What is orange? Why an orange
Just an orange.

Jack Hodgkinson (10)
Wellesbourne School, Norris Green

What Is Pink?
(Based on 'What Is Pink?' by Christina Rossetti)

What is pink? Cheeks are pink
While you wash your face in the sink.
What is red? Roses are red
While they lie in their flower bed.
What is blue? The sea is blue
Watch the waves travel through.
What is white? Clouds are white
You can see them in the light.
What is yellow? The sun is yellow
Shining down on the little fellow.
What is green? A crocodile is green
Watch it swim through the stream.
What is violet? Part of a rainbow is violet.
Higher than an aeroplane can go with a pilot.
What is orange? Honey is orange
Just ordinary honey.

Nathan Goldby (10)
Wellesbourne School, Norris Green

What Is Pink?
(Based on 'What Is Pink?' by Christina Rossetti)

What is pink? A flamingo is pink
But not when it's covered in ink.
What is red? A rose is red
But only its head.
What is blue? The sky is blue
The one, which is above you.
What is white? Paper's white
You can make a paper kite.
What is green? Our school jumpers are green
And the teachers are mean.
What is violet? Plums are violet
Growing in the twilight.
What is orange? Why an orange.
Just an orange.

Loni Crossland (10)
Wellesbourne School, Norris Green

What Is Pink?
(Based on 'What Is Pink?' by Christina Rossetti)

What is pink? Blossom is pink
Where it hangs over the River Link
What is red? Strawberries are red
Growing in their compost bed.
What is blue? The sea is blue
Just like bluebells all day through.
What is white? Stars are white
That makes the sky shine all night.
What is yellow? The sun is yellow
It makes your face look very mellow
What is green? Leaves are green
Just like apples nice and clean
What is violet? Violets are violet
In the twilight.
What is orange? A pepper is orange
A nice, juicy, orange pepper.

Francesca Davies (10)
Wellesbourne School, Norris Green

What Is Pink?
(Based on 'What Is Pink?' by Christina Rossetti)

What is pink? Paint is pink
It often dries as quick as a wink.
What is red? Blood is red
Flowing in your veins to your head.
What is blue? Everton is blue
Friendly people playing football too.
What is white? Teeth are white
Shining brightly in the light.
What is yellow? Bananas are yellow
Delicious mashed up with a marshmallow.
What is green? A mint is green
When I eat it I seem to gleam.
What is violet? Flowers are violet.
Their scent drifting in the sky.
What is orange? Paper is orange
Just a piece of orange paper.

Lisa Roberts (10)
Wellesbourne School, Norris Green

What Is Pink?
(Based on 'What Is Pink?' by Christina Rossetti)

What is pink? Our lips are pink
To drink the water from our sink.
What is red? Roses are red
Swaying gently in their bed.
What is blue? Veins are blue
With out blood passing through.
What is white? Stars are white
Twinkling really, really bright.
What is yellow? The sun is yellow
What a great and friendly fellow.
What is green? Trees are green
Standing tall and very lean.
What is violet? Flowers are violet
That looks nice in the light.
What is orange? A mango is orange
Just an orange mango.

Georgina Jarrold (11)
Wellesbourne School, Norris Green

What Is Pink?
(Based on 'What Is Pink?' by Christina Rossetti)

What is pink? Pigs are pink
And very often they really stink.
What is red? A rose is red
A rose that is lying on a bed
What is blue? My dad's old shoe is blue
It's held together with some strong glue
What is white? A kite is white
Flying in the sky so bright.
What is yellow? A lemon is yellow
A bitter taste for any fellow
What is green? Peas are green
They seem to make my sister mean.
What is violet? My mum's room is violet
Just like the flowers that grow in the woods.
What is orange? My quilt is orange
My cosy orange quilt.

Kyle Hesketh (10)
Wellesbourne School, Norris Green

What Is Pink?
(Based on 'What Is Pink?' by Christina Rossetti)

What is pink? A pig is pink
And sometimes they really stink
What is red? A rose is red
When it's not watered then it's dead.
What is blue? Your veins are blue
Where your blood runs right through.
What is white? The clouds are white
Sailing through the sky like a kite.
What is yellow? The sun is yellow
It shines down on the meadow.
What is green? Trees are green
Standing tall and very lean.
What is violet? Flowers are violet
Growing in the meadow.
What is orange? A tangerine is orange
Just a tangerine!

Ashley Chiocchi (10)
Wellesbourne School, Norris Green

What Is Pink?
(Based on 'What Is Pink?' by Christina Rossetti)

What is pink? Flowers are pink
Where water sometimes sinks
What is red? LFC is red
Maybe the colour of your bed.
What is blue? Everton is blue
We all cheer when a goal goes through.
What is white? Bones are white
Maybe they make picture on your kite.
What is yellow? Sand is yellow
It blows on a fellow.
What is green? Grass is green.
Green like a long, stringy bean
What is violet? Violet is the colour of clouds.
That float through the sky
What is orange? The sun is orange
Just an orange sun.

Joe Chiocchi (10)
Wellesbourne School, Norris Green

What Is Pink?
(Based on 'What Is Pink?' by Christina Rossetti)

What is pink? Flowers are pink
Waiting for water from the sink.
What is red? LFC are red,
Playing football then going to bed.
What is blue? The ocean is blue,
With the waves going through.
What is white? Your teeth are white
Getting cleaned every night.
What is yellow? Bananas are yellow,
Being munched in a clear meadow
What is green? Leaves are green.
Floating to the ground with flowers in-between.
What is violet? Violets are violet,
Growing bigger every week.
What is orange? Sunsets are orange,
Just orange sunsets!

Lauren Fox (10)
Wellesbourne School, Norris Green

What Is Pink?
(Based on 'What Is Pink?' by Christina Rossetti)

What is pink? Lips are pink
Baby lips waiting to have a drink.
What is red? Strawberries are red
Like growing roses in a flower bed.
What is blue? The sea is blue.
With lots of boats floating through.
What is white? Daisies are white
Dancing like fairies through the light
What is yellow? A melon is yellow
It's nice and juicy and mellow.
What is green? The leaves are green
Just like apples crisp and clean.
What is violet? Violets are violet
Growing like jewels when the world is silent.
What is orange? A pepper is orange
A lovely, shiny, orange pepper.

Alisha Roberts (11)
Wellesbourne School, Norris Green

What Is Pink?
(Based on 'What Is Pink?' by Christina Rossetti)

What is pink? Cheeks are pink
You wash them in the sink.
What is red? Blood is red
It flows around in your head.
What is blue? Everton is blue
Everyone likes to watch them play too.
What is white? Paint is white
It makes your room nice and bright.
What is yellow? A banana is yellow
With a taste that is cool and mellow.
What is green? Grass is green
Opening a meadow into a lovely scene.
What is violet? A rainbow is violet
As bright as a light.
What is orange? A peach is orange
Just a lovely peach.

Stephen McKee (10)
Wellesbourne School, Norris Green

What Is Pink?
(Based on 'What Is Pink?' by Christina Rossetti)

What is pink? A pig is pink
Rolling in the mud with a blink
What is red? Strawberries are red
Growing in the muddy shed
What is blue? The sea is blue
The sea flowing over you
What is white? The snow is white
Falling down with a kite
What is yellow? The sun is yellow
Shining down at the meadow
What is green? Leaves are green
Falling down to the stream
What is violet? A flower is violet
Growing and growing in the light
What is orange? The sunset is orange
Just the sunset.

Matthew Provost (10)
Wellesbourne School, Norris Green

What Is Pink?
(Based on 'What Is Pink?' by Christina Rossetti)

What is pink? A rose is pink
Cut off the end and write with ink!
What is red? Fruit stains are red
When a baby has just been fed!
What is blue? The sky is blue
It's the right place for you two!
What is white? A dove is white
Flying higher than a kite!
What is yellow? Bananas are yellow
When they are fresh and mellow!
What is green? A kiwi is green
When it is soft and clean!
What is violet? Pansies are violet
Sparkling in the twilight!
What is orange? Why an orange
Just an orange!

Natasha Wright (10)
Wellesbourne School, Norris Green

What Is Pink?
(Based on 'What Is Pink?' by Christina Rossetti)

What is pink? A flamingo is pink
But something makes it stink.
What is red? Blood is red,
Mostly when someone is dead.
What is blue? The sky is blue
As ducks flew.
What is white? Swans are white
They fly out of your sight.
What is yellow? Lemons are yellow
And some people bellow.
What is green? Apples are green
And sometimes they are not to be seen.
What is violet? Bluebells are violet
And can be seen by a pilot.
What is orange? Why, an orange.
Just an orange!

Steven Lambert (10)
Wellesbourne School, Norris Green

What Is Pink?
(Based on 'What Is Pink?' by Christina Rossetti)

What is pink? A pig is pink,
And all it does is wink.
What is red? Blood is red
From people who are dead.
What is blue? The sky is blue
The colour of you.
What is white? The clouds are white
And they are awfully bright.
What is yellow? A daffodil is yellow,
And when the wind blows it's mellow.
What is green? A crocodile is green,
And it is very mean.
What is violet? The sunset is violet.
In the summer twilight.
What is orange? Why an orange
Just an orange.

Alex Walker (10)
Wellesbourne School, Norris Green

What Is Pink?
(Based on 'What Is Pink?' by Christina Rossetti)

What is pink? A balloon is pink
Which will not sink.
What is red? Hair is red
Which stays on your head.
What is blue? The pool is blue
Like the man's shoe.
What is white? A sheet is white
And you can see it in the night.
What is yellow? The sun is yellow
Making heat through the meadow
What is green? Seaweed's green
With little fish swimming in-between.
What is violet? Bluebells are violet
Like the bright skylight.
What is orange? Why an orange
Just an orange.

Kyle Newby (10)
Wellesbourne School, Norris Green

What Is Pink?
(Based on 'What Is Pink?' by Christina Rossetti)

What is pink? A rose is pink
To make the boys wink!
What is red? Blood is red
When you are laying in the dead!
What is blue? The sky is blue
It's just the place for you!
What is white? A dove is white
It is just like the light!
What is yellow? A flower is yellow
And it says 'Hello!'
What is green? A kiwi is green
When it is nice and green
What is violet? A sunset is violet
Drifting in the skylight!
What is orange? Why an orange
Just an orange.

Gemma Bishop (11)
Wellesbourne School, Norris Green

What Is Pink?
(Based on 'What Is Pink?' by Christina Rossetti)

What is pink? Toilet rolls are pink
It might even stink.
What is red? Hair is red
It might even be on someone's head
What is blue? A jumper is blue
Even if it's new.
What is white? Clouds are white
They can even be so bright.
What is yellow? Birds are yellow
And they can even bellow.
What is green? An apple is green
But it's got to be clean
What is violet? The sunset is violet
Next to it is a pilot
What is orange? Why an orange
Just an orange!

Jake Riley (10)
Wellesbourne School, Norris Green

What Is Pink?
(Based on 'What Is Pink?' by Christina Rossetti)

What is pink? A pig is pink,
Which let out a rather big stink
What is red? A rose is red
In its flowery bed
What is blue? The sky is blue
Where the clouds follow through
What is white? A dove is white
Sailing in the sparkly skylight
What is yellow? Daffodils are yellow
Peaceful, calm and mellow
What is green? The grass is green
Grazing through the scene
What is violet? Bluebells are violet
Calmly in the twilight
What is orange? Why an orange
Just an orange.

Laura Gladwinfield (10)
Wellesbourne School, Norris Green

What Is Pink?
(Based on 'What Is Pink?' by Christina Rossetti)

What is pink? A pig is pink
Smelling with such a stink
What is red? A rose is red
Sitting by its flower bed
What is blue? The sky
Looking down on you
What is white? A swan is
White as swans through the night
What is yellow? Daffodils are yellow
Sitting there relaxed and mellow
What is green? An apple is green
Juicy and clean
What is violet? Bluebells are violet
Upon the summer twilight.
What is orange? Why an orange?
Just an orange!

Laura Teare (10)
Wellesbourne School, Norris Green

What Is Pink?
(Based on 'What Is Pink?' by Christina Rossetti)

What is pink? A pig is pink
Which has a horrible stink
What is red? Any bed is red
The colour when I cut my head
What is blue? The sky is blue
The colour of my shoe
What is white? My bread is white
When I take a juicy bite
What is yellow? Bananas are yellow
Which are very ripe and mellow.
What is green? Grass is green
Even though it isn't clean.
What is violet? The clouds are violet
Like the suit on the pilot
What is orange? Why an orange
Just an orange.

Jordan Lamb (10)
Wellesbourne School, Norris Green

What Is Pink?
(Based on 'What Is Pink?' by Christina Rossetti)

What is pink? A blossom is pink
It makes me blink.
What is red? A rose is red
When you never feed it, it is dead.
What is blue? The sea is blue
Where the sailing boats float through.
What is white? The clouds are white
Gliding past the light.
What is yellow? The sun is yellow
Shining down on the meadow.
What is green? The grass is green
With mini flowers in-between.
What is violet? Aeroplanes are violet
Driven by a pilot.
What is orange? A tangerine is orange
Just a tangerine.

Wesley Cave (10)
Wellesbourne School, Norris Green

My Dog

Oh how I love my dog
It's like a fluffy pillow in the night,
She kisses me when I am down,
She is like a best friend that you never fall out with.
She is never cheerless, she is always playful,
She never wants to go she is all I could ever wish for.
If I lose her I will never know what to do.
She is as friendly as the morning sun,
She is my best friend, oh how I love her and I always will.

Danielle Jamieson (11)
Woodlands Primary School, Birkenhead

Going Away

I look up in the sun
Feeling all alone
Because my phone hasn't rung
I feel all worried but I keep it inside as I have a lot to hide.

I feel the wind I feel the breeze
I wish I could have the happiness that I need.

When he left me on my own
It tore me apart and broke my heart
Instead of in the cold earth on his own
That bit of my heart would be back in place
If he was still here.

Lindsay Watson (10)
Woodlands Primary School, Birkenhead

Darkness

It creeps up behind you
But you never know when
It dashes to get you,
But you never can tell
When darkness will strike
It can hide in the shadows
Or under your bed
But sometimes darkness
Is just inside your head.

Masuma Begum (10)
Woodlands Primary School, Birkenhead

Happiness

Happiness is like the sunshine
Coming out from the clouds
Happiness is like the world
Going round and round
Happiness is like the bright
Sun shining down on me
Happiness is like the lovely
Things that I can see
Happiness takes away
All the bad things that have
Happened in my life
Happiness is the greatest feeling.

Nicole Hartley (10)
Woodlands Primary School, Birkenhead